What others [...] Coach Yow and [...]

The moment I heard about this compilation of personal insights from Wolfpack players about their experiences with Coach Kay Yow, I thought to myself, "Wow, I cannot wait to get my hands on this book!" These unique life lessons not only show the powerful role of a coach and player relationship, but they also show the impact that a phenomenal coach such as Kay Yow can truly have on a student-athlete. She undoubtedly personified the DNA that makes up an extraordinary coach, both on and off the court.

Beth Bass, CEO, Women's Basketball Coaches Association (WBCA)

Times do change, but Kay Yow remained the same charming and caring person we all loved so dearly. She always made you feel important to her, if not to anyone else. I was so glad that I went to Dallas, Texas in 2008 to play in the 4Kay Golf Classic. Coach Yow will always be remembered by me and everyone she befriended. I am one of the lucky ones who could call her a close, personal friend.

Orlando "Tubby" Smith, Head Coach, Minnesota Basketball

Throughout her 30-plus years on the sideline, Coach Kay Yow never lost sight of the two things she deemed most important: faith and people. The common thread of her commitment to serve God and love people weaves throughout these poignant stories from Wolfpack players, reminding us that an extraordinary life is defined more by loving people well than by winning games.

Sue Semrau, Head Coach, Florida State Women's Basketball

Kay Yow was a very successful basketball coach but more importantly, a special leader and teacher. She earned the respect of all who knew her by trying to make those around her better rather than focusing on herself. She may have been a hall of fame coach but what I admired was how she prepared her players for life after basketball.

Nick Valvano, CEO, The V Foundation

Coach Yow was one of those rare coaches who helped her athletes become more than just better basketball players. She captured the heart of an athlete and inspired her to become the woman God created her to be. Her story, so lovingly told by her players, is a testimony to a life well lived.

Donna Noonan, Director of Coaches Ministry, FCA

Kay's life and work as a coach and mentor influenced, shaped and offered life lessons to countless people across America. This wonderful book shares the depth and wide scope of that influence on some of those she impacted the most in her career. It is an inspiring read.

Debbie Yow, Director of Athletics, University of Maryland

This is a great read on how one person can powerfully impact the life of another when we place our life's endeavors in the hands of our Lord and Savior Jesus Christ. You will be encouraged and challenged to live a life that counts for others.

Susan Yow, Head Coach, Belmont Abbey Women's Basketball

Coach Yow touched so many lives. Her genuine love for people was an outpouring of her love for Jesus. She had incredible leadership skills: character, passion, vision, thoughtfulness, playfulness and love. God armored her with a persistence that has inspired millions. You, too, will be inspired by reading how God chose Coach Yow to lead the Pack.

Faith Mimnaugh, Head Coach, Cal Poly Women's Basketball

Kay was who most of us in coaching aspire to be. She was funny, warm, bold, generous—and a great coach. What an example she was to us all. Everyone should read *Leader of the Pack* to experience the inspiration and wisdom of this wonderful woman of God.

Nancy Wilson, Head Coach, College of Charleston Women's Basketball

Coach Yow's friendship and leadership touched us in special and everlasting ways. Her gifts of wisdom, kindness and love remain with us, continuing to challenge and inspire. Through grace she lights our way.

Herb Sendek, Head Coach, Arizona State Basketball

LEADER
OF THE
PACK

THE LEGACY OF LEGENDARY COACH KAY YOW

STEPHANIE ZONARS

CONTENTS

Wolfpack Influence

Acknowledgements

The journey of compiling and writing *Leader of the Pack* had multiple stops and involved many people. First and foremost I thank Coach Yow herself for allowing me the privilege of contributing to her written legacy. In life and even in death, she never missed an opportunity to point people to God–may this book do the same.

To the members of the Wolfpack women's basketball family who submitted stories–you've given the world a unique perspective of Coach Yow. Through your eyes we see the reasons why she was such a remarkable woman and a one-in-a-million coach. Thank you for sharing your memories. May they allow her life to touch and inspire thousands more!

To Stephanie Glance–your valuable insights along the way were imperative the completion of this book and so appreciated. Thank you for your guidance and perspective.

To Claudia Kreicker Dozier–thank you for believing in this idea from its inception, for writing the first story and for your feedback on the rough draft. Your prayers and encouragement at each crucial step helped keep me going.

To Judy Kirkpatrick and Natalie Nuce–thank you for your encouragement throughout the process and your input on the final manuscript. Invaluable!

To Ronnie Yow–the family photos you provided make this book extra special. Family was always more important to Coach Yow than coaching, and the photos of her life away from the court make that so clear. Thank you.

To Sandra Bishop and MacGregor Literary–thank you for your belief in this project and your efforts to find the perfect publishing home for it.

To Karl DeBlaker–your photos of Coach Yow remind us not only of her accomplishments but of all the qualities that made her so dear. Your creative gift adds a special element to this book. Thank you.

To my friends and family who encouraged me repeatedly throughout this writing journey–thank you for not tiring of listening to the details and for sticking with me until the end. I am grateful!

And more than any other, to Jesus–this book was your idea. May it cause every reader's heart to turn toward you again, or for the very first time.

Dedicated to the memory of Coach Kay Yow,
Thank you for inspiring me and so many others
to love God and people,
to walk in humility and
to never give up.

Foreword

I had the privilege and wonderful blessing of working with Coach Kay Yow for 15 years. Serving as her associate head coach, I gleaned many timeless lessons from her as she lived out biblical principles in her everyday life. When approached about the idea of a book consisting of lessons former players learned from her connected to corresponding biblical principles, she was receptive only because she thought perhaps others may benefit in some way. That showed her truest heart–Coach Yow was always about helping others!

One of the most respected coaches in the U.S. and abroad, Kay Yow spent a lifetime putting others before herself and trying to make a small difference in their lives. Her humility, grace and wisdom constantly shone through her daily actions and interactions, touching and influencing every person blessed to cross her path. Her reserved personality combined with her faithful spirit and ever-prevailing servant's heart made her a mentor to many and a friend to all.

Watching her battle cancer for more than 20 years with courage, grace and dignity, one could only imagine what strong faith lie beneath that rock-solid exterior. That faith anchored her life, helping her to both see and speak of the blessings she experienced as a result of cancer. She always saw the glass half-full and the silver lining in every dark cloud, exemplifying positivity at its highest point through sayings like:

When life kicks you, let it kick you forward.

Don't wallow in self-pity, you'll drown.
Just swish your feet a little and get out!

We have little or no control over what happens to us in life,
but we have 100% control over how we will respond!

The way she lived her life and the lessons she imparted to us serve as a well of strength, perseverance, hope, faith and love that we can draw from forever. So if you face adversity and struggle to find hope, you will certainly find encouragement from the spiritual truths woven throughout the pages of this book, as well as from the sampling of stories shared by three decades of former players whose lives were deeply touched by their phenomenal, inspiring leader. Just as our lives were richer for having known her, so too will your life be blessed by reading her story and understanding her faith.

Thank you, Coach Yow, for sharing your life and wisdom with us and for leaving an indelible imprint on our hearts and in our minds. Most of all, thank you for sharing your faith and giving us a godly example of how to live each day to its fullest, responding humbly in victory and gratefully in defeat. You were an amazing inspiration to us all!

Stephanie Glance
NC State Associate Head Coach
1994-2009

Preface

To those who knew her, thoughts of Coach Kay Yow bring to mind a long list of superlatives, many of which are strewn throughout the stories in this book. Yet to me, four words best summarize her time on earth: *A life well-lived.*

A life well-lived isn't calculated by the number of championships, victories or hall of fame inductions. In fact, it's not a calculation at all. A life well-lived happens when one knows and fulfills her God-given purpose, leaving life-changing imprints on people's hearts along the way. Though all of us hope to look back one day and use those same four words to describe our lives, many don't know how to get there. Coach Yow gave us a great example to follow.

"Living successfully beats becoming successful," she once said. As one of just a few Division I women's basketball coaches to win over 700 games, Coach Yow understood what it felt like to become successful. But to her, living successfully held an even higher importance. And from her perspective the ability to live successfully began with dedicating her life to God.

On January 19, 1976 Coach Yow set aside time for a Campus Crusade for Christ staff member to meet with her NC State team. Upon hearing how she could have a personal relationship with God, she prayed and asked Christ to take charge of her life. This ignited a desire to know and obey him, leading her on a faith journey that would come to define her life.

Initially, this book was to be a compilation of stories written by Wolfpack players that described Coach Yow's influence on their lives. But Coach Yow expanded on that idea, requesting that I write an entry connecting each player story to wisdom from the Bible. Coach Yow knew she wasn't perfect, but those imperfections drove her to Christ, who embraced her with forgiveness, grace and mercy. And so, the cry of her heart was that as you turn each page you would see not her life, but Christ's life in her.

Above all, Coach Yow wanted *Leader of the Pack* to reflect the credit for her success (in both basketball and in life) back to the God who guided her every step of the way. As a result, each chapter includes Wolfpack History (stories submitted by various Wolfpack players) along with Wolfpack Wisdom (my entry that ties the player story to wisdom from the Bible). At the end, you'll also find Wolfpack Influence–stories submitted by college coaches whose lives were richer for having known Coach Yow.

Enjoy the history of one of the strongest traditions in women's basketball. Learn from the wisdom of a seasoned college coach. But most of all, find inspiration for your own journey from a life well-lived.

Stephanie Zonars
June 2009

1

In the Beginning

Genie Jordan Ussery
NC State Wolfpack, 1971-1975

WOLFPACK HISTORY

Excitement filled the air in 1974-75 when a group of young, collegiate women at NC State finally became an official varsity team within the athletic department. Several of us had played on the club basketball team the last few years, and I was one of a few seniors. I never dreamed that my participation on this team would introduce me to an icon in the world of women's sports.

In the spring of 1975 the athletics council met to decide who to recommend to then athletic director, Willis Casey, to fill the position of women's basketball coach. Peanut Doak graciously took the job for the 1974-75 season on an interim basis until a full search could be conducted. As one of two student-athletes on campus with a seat on the athletic council, I vividly remember the meeting in Talley when we unanimously recommended Coach Kay Yow, then the head coach at Elon College. Coach Yow had already made a name for herself, not only by her team's winning records, but also by the manner in which her teams played and she coached.

The thrill and honor of having served as a co-captain of the first collegiate women's basketball team at NC State was diminished only by the realization that I would never play for this coaching legend. My senior year, I played against her Elon team and the following year, as a women's basketball graduate assistant at UNC-Chapel Hill, I again observed Coach Yow–this time with her at the helm on my beloved NC State soil–and could easily see that the Wolfpack was in GREAT hands.

The journey of women's participation in collegiate athletics, although greatly aided by Title IX, has been an arduous one. Coach Yow served as God's instrument in the world of women's athletics, consistently demonstrating three qualities necessary for sustained growth: determination, loyalty and patience.

Determination means staying the course regardless of the opposition. Coach Yow purposed to accomplish God's goals in God's timing. I can't count the number of varied circumstances I watched her face with a never-give-up attitude. Whether on the court or in her personal life, she constantly reflected a determined spirit. *Loyalty* means demonstrating a commitment to God and to those he's called us to serve, even in difficult circumstances. Coach Yow resisted pride and remained loyal to NC State for over 30 years, continuing to work hard even in times when her program didn't receive what she felt it deserved. *Patience* means accepting a difficult situation from God without giving him a deadline to remove it. Professionally, personally and especially in her fight against cancer, Coach Yow reflected a patient spirit and a willingness to be still and know that he is God.

I feel honored to have called Coach Yow a friend. Her virtue and integrity made Wolfpack women one of the most blessed groups of women on this earth. Although I never played under her I am grateful for a friendship built on our two common loves: Jesus Christ and NC State women's basketball.

WOLFPACK WISDOM

Be still, and know that I am God! I will be honored by every nation. I will be honored throughout the world.

Psalm 46:10

In our fast-paced, western society, we might mistake the "stillness" of Psalm 46 to be a call for physical inactivity. It more accurately refers, however, to an attitude of stillness—of ceasing to strive. An internal state saturated by faith in the one true God and by knowledge of his overwhelming power. Ceasing to strive, both internally and externally, allows us to see the beauty and power of how God brings all things together for the good of those who love him.[1] Knowing that he is God reminds us that we don't have to force life, but can trust him to bring about his plans in his time. We learn how to walk *with* him, not ahead or behind, and as we do he produces in us qualities like determination, loyalty and patience to help us on the journey.

Perhaps no person in Bible times reflects the understanding of "ceasing to strive" better than Joseph.[2] Born the youngest of twelve sons, Joseph found favor with his father Jacob—and his brothers hated him for it. Joseph added fuel to that hatred when he told his brothers about a dream God gave him in which they bowed down to him.

If Joseph thought the pathway to power would be easy because God ordained it, he quickly learned otherwise. His journey resembled an old, dirt mountain road laden with rocks, potholes and curves. Circumstances at every turn challenged his faith, likely causing him to wonder how he would ever be given a position of authority over anyone, let alone his brothers. With the same qualities Genie saw in Coach Yow, Joseph determined to follow God, to show loyalty to those in authority over him and to live patiently in obscurity until God raised him up.

When Joseph's brothers first plotted to kill him and then instead sold him into slavery, he had to wonder how this fit into the dream

God had given him. Opposition elicits either hesitation or determination. Surely he experienced moments of hesitation, confused by his circumstances, yet the Scriptures say "The Lord was with Joseph"[3]–something that even his master, Potiphar noticed. Though his circumstances didn't make sense, God's presence remained with Joseph, bringing him success in everything he did. This earned him favor with Potiphar, who soon put Joseph in charge of everything he owned. Joseph proved his determination to walk with God no matter what obstacles he faced. Unfortunately, more were on the way.

Just when things were looking up, Potiphar's wife began uttering seductive words to entice Joseph to sleep with her. Some scholars say her attempts went on not just for days, but for years. Joseph endured this harassment, modeling steadfast loyalty to his master as he continuously refused her advances. Eventually, she grew so frustrated that she framed him, accusing him of rape and landing him in jail. This turn of events would send most people into a downward spiral of bitterness and anger. After all, how would Joseph's dream ever come to pass when he continued to be the victim of injustice? But because the Lord was with him, Joseph resisted a pity party and soon became the warden's favorite, in charge of everything in the jail. Even when his dream got derailed, Joseph remained loyal to those in authority over him.

Later, when Pharaoh threw his chief cup-bearer and baker in jail, they requested that Joseph interpret their dreams. The cup-bearer's dream meant he would one day be restored to his position with the king, so Joseph asked him to remind Pharaoh that he was still locked up in jail awaiting release. The cup-bearer's dream came true just as Joseph had said, but upon being restored to his position with the king, he forgot about Joseph for two long years. Once again, the dream seemed so improbable. But Joseph remained faithful to the warden and patiently waited for God to bring his dream to fruition.

Finally, when Pharaoh needed a dream interpreted, the cup-bearer remembered Joseph. Upon hearing the interpretation, Pharaoh was so impressed with Joseph's spirit-filled wisdom and intelligence that he placed him in charge of the entire land of Egypt, and Joseph's dream became reality.

Both Joseph and Coach Yow walked their journeys with determination, loyalty and patience made possible by God's undeniable presence. At each mile marker along the way, the Lord was with Joseph and the Lord was with Coach Yow. As they leaned into him, learning how to trust with stilled hearts, he gave them strength to pursue the dream, stay the course and never give up.

2

Adopted into the Family

Donna Andrews
NC State Wolfpack, 1975-1977

WOLFPACK HISTORY

I was already enrolled at NC State in 1975 when Kay Yow was hired as the head coach of the Wolfpack women's basketball team. I felt privileged to play not only basketball, but also volleyball under Coach Yow's guidance and leadership.

She faced an uphill battle from the very first day–lack of facilities, Title IX, and limited scholarship monies–but it never diminished her enthusiasm and vision for the program. We pioneered collegiate women's sports without the amenities that athletes enjoy today. Without a locker room, we used the ROTC room in Reynolds Coliseum or we changed in our dorm rooms. Our pre-game meal consisted of whatever we could find on campus. We washed our own uniforms after games and got excited if more than 100 fans filled the stands. Nonetheless, I wouldn't trade one minute of my Wolfpack basketball experience. The opportunity to help lay the foundation for NC State women's basketball and to play for Coach Yow was priceless.

One cold and snowy night in January 1977, we played the Mighty Macs from Immaculata. At half-time we trailed by 20 points. The fans didn't expect much from us against such a storied program, and dismissed our chances to win. Yet we had someone on our side that the Mighty Macs did not–Coach Yow. She never gave up on us and we rallied to send the game into overtime. Though we lost by five, our comeback proved our team's resilience, not to mention Coach Yow's never-say-die attitude.

Coach Yow taught me about TEAM. I learned how to be a team

player and to lead by example. She coached using encouraging words laced with constructive critique, pushing each player to reach her potential on and off the court. By consistently modeling integrity, character, responsibility, attitude and accountability, she provided a living example of qualities I've sought to emulate throughout my entire adult life.

Once a player donned the Wolfpack uniform, she was forever a part of Coach Yow's family—not just in word, but in deed. Whether speaking at a youth volunteer coaches banquet in Hickory, NC or attending my father's funeral, Coach Yow was always there. She walked with me through health issues—even while she battled her own cancer for the third time—reminding me to persevere and to never give up. Whether in laughter or tears, I treasured every moment we shared. Coach Yow will always be the *Leader of the Pack*, and she made me and many others so proud to be part of the Wolfpack family.

WOLFPACK WISDOM

God decided in advance to adopt us into his own family by bringing us to himself through Jesus Christ. This is what he wanted to do, and it gave him great pleasure.

Ephesians 1:5

In 1964 Coach Yow set out to become the best basketball coach she could be. Daily she went about her work in the only way she knew how–by treating people with respect, by working hard and by pursuing excellence. Though she never married or had biological children, she mothered hundreds of young women. At NC State, Coach Yow adopted each of her players into the Wolfpack family, and she took that adoption seriously. A remarkable, tight-knit, intensely loyal group of Wolfpack women formed–a natural result of the little things she did every day to serve, love and care for her players. Signing to play for the Wolfpack meant so much more than wearing a jersey on game day. It meant receiving the benefits of adoption into the Wolfpack family–for life.

Adopt literally means "to make one's own by selection or assent."[4] People across the globe adopt children whose parents can't care for them, or perhaps died as a result of illness or war. Imagine a child's joy in being chosen! Every child desires the security of a loving family and when children in hopeless situations receive that gift, it changes everything.

In a spiritual sense, every human heart desires the same thing–love, security and a home for our soul. Though since birth our fallen nature has separated us from God, it brings him pleasure to adopt us into his family.

But when the right time came, God sent his Son, born of a woman, subject to the law. God sent him to buy freedom for us who were slaves to the law, so that he could adopt us as his very own children. And because we are his children, God has sent the Spirit of his Son into our hearts, prompting us to call out, "Abba, Father." Now you are no longer a slave but God's own child. And since you are his child, God has made you his heir. (Galatians 4:4-7)

Jesus purchased our freedom, making it possible for us to be adopted into God's family. When we receive that gift by faith, we experience all the benefits of being God's child—forever. Like an adopted child who inherits the same rights and privileges as her parent's biological children, so those adopted into God's family become heirs and gain the right to share in Jesus' inheritance.[5] God guarantees this inheritance—eternity in heaven—by placing his Spirit within us:

And when you believed in Christ, he identified you as his own by giving you the Holy Spirit, whom he promised long ago. The Spirit is God's guarantee that he will give us the inheritance he promised and that he has purchased us to be his own people. He did this so we would praise and glorify him. (Ephesians 1:13b-14)

Talk about security! A trustworthy God who cannot lie assures those who place their faith in him a priceless inheritance that can never spoil or fade.[6] Adoption into God's family changes everything. No matter our past, we receive the hope, security and love our soul thirsts for, as well as a Father who will never abandon us.

Coach Yow created a similar kind of adoptive family. Once a young woman received the invitation to play at NC State, life changed. Regardless of her background or family situation, she now became part of the Wolfpack family. She realized this family wasn't just about basketball by the way Coach Yow served, loved and cared for her not only as an athlete, but also as a student and person—even long after she'd left campus. If she knew anything, it was that Coach Yow cared. Personalized, birthday and Christmas cards, phone calls and visits showed that when Coach Yow adopted her, it was for life. No wonder that on Alumni Weekend 2007, nearly all the Wolfpack women from the last three decades gathered to tell their "mom" how much their adoption meant to them. They knew they were still part of the family.

3

Authentic Greatness

Sherri Pickard
NC State Wolfpack, 1975-1977

WOLFPACK HISTORY

I began my college career at Elon College in 1973 because I wanted to play for Coach Kay Yow. Times were different back then for female athletes. We used the old track team warm-ups, drove our own cars to games and stayed four to a room whenever we needed a hotel. My sophomore year the cafeteria provided us with box lunches for some of our away games for the first time. What grand memories–every girl on the team truly wanted to be there with Coach Yow, a pioneer who daily fought for our opportunity to participate and compete.

That summer, the Russian National team toured the U.S. and several regional All-Star teams were selected to play them. I participated on one of those teams, with Coach Yow serving as our coach. This marked the first time that the Russians played women's basketball in the U.S., so it garnered lots of publicity and was one of the highlights of my athletic career. Coach Yow exuded her usual optimistic, enthusiastic self, so as players we didn't realize that no one gave us a chance of winning the game. In the locker room before the game, she gave us a goal of scoring 40 points. I, of course, thought that meant we'd hold the Russians to less than 40 points! They beat us 114-41, but we accomplished our goal! Coach Yow made sure we understood that the magnitude of the event encompassed much more than the game itself. It represented an opportunity to meet people from another country, make new friends, learn new customs, play before a sell-out crowd...and score more than 40 points. The score was just one part of the whole–it did not define us!

When Coach Yow took the job at NC State, I went with her because I knew I had been blessed with an amazing opportunity. Coach Yow's perpetual energy, commitment and work ethic demanded, in a gentle way, the same from each of us. Her enthusiasm for each sport, event and athlete infected every player, instilling in us an overwhelming determination to not disappoint her. She never yelled or berated, yet any of us would have run through a wall for her. And I believe she would have done the same for us!

She prepared us well for every opponent, making it easy for us to focus and perform. We enjoyed each other and the camaraderie of being Wolfpack women. Coach Yow's daily enthusiasm, preparation, support and 100% commitment taught us that success happens one day at a time and that every day is defined by the effort put into it. We didn't always win, but we knew that she would be back out there the next day, enthusiastic, prepared and giving her all. She constantly sought the next level in an attempt to make us better through a new drill, a new explanation of a necessary technique or an inspiring quote. Quietly and with unrelenting patience she encouraged us to keep pushing. One more time–one more time–one more time!

Even though I played for Coach Yow in the mid-70's, I didn't fully grasp her authentic greatness until Alumni Weekend 2007. The depth of her impact on my life is so profound that it took me that long to understand it. But that February night, with 110 of her 125 Wolfpack players present, I got it! I stood in the back of the room, watching player after player from the 70's, 80's, 90's, and 2000's speak–some with tears, some with humor, but all with a sincerity that touched my heart. I looked around with acute awareness of this amazing family that Kay Yow had created for all of us through her commitment, dedication, perseverance, graciousness and loyalty. All these special, unique and talented women and their families had been impacted by this woman and her gift–what a privilege to be part of it!

This Alumni Weekend took on a sense of urgency since Coach Yow's cancer had returned with such force. Everyone wondered if this was the last time our Wolfpack family would gather with Coach Yow at the center. As player after player searched for the words to articulate what Coach Yow meant to her, I realized the inadequacy of words when trying to describe how someone has not only touched, but changed me. There she sat–my mentor, my teacher, my coach, the most significant role model in my life–it was impossible to imagine a world without her in it. Since I was 15 years old, Coach Yow had been a fixture in my life and my heart, a beacon of light providing guidance as I navigated through the world. Her example and willingness to share her faith led me to make the most important decision of my life–to accept Jesus Christ as my personal savior.

I spoke that night as a prodigal who has come and gone, but who always felt welcomed to return. As I have chased my dreams (and a few rabbits), one thought remained in the back of my mind: would she be proud of me? Why does it matter so much if she would be proud of me? Even all these years later, I still don't want to disappoint her.

WOLFPACK WISDOM

You have heard me teach things that have been confirmed by many reliable witnesses. Now teach these truths to other trustworthy people who will be able to pass them on to others.

2 Timothy 2:2

Coach Yow left fingerprints all over the game of women's basketball. She pioneered the program at NC State where the halls of Reynolds Coliseum and the court which bears her name still echo with the enthusiasm, passion and integrity she used to build the Wolfpack women into perennial national contenders. Hall of fame inductions, Olympic gold medals, records galore along with virtually every accolade a coach could achieve–Coach Yow garnered them all.

Although these accomplishments comprise part of her legacy, Coach Yow would be utterly disappointed if her remembrance didn't extend beyond the trophy case. In fact, she would probably nix the awards altogether in order to be remembered for the other, more meaningful part of her legacy–the one that lives on in the hearts of her players, staff and the thousands she touched. Coach Yow knew the secret to a lasting legacy began and ended with relationships. She invested her whole life in teaching women principles imperative to living successfully. Principles that, because they worked, have been passed on from the Wolfpack women to parents, husbands, children and many others.

The apostle Paul also understood that the road to a lasting legacy is paved with meaningful relationships. After becoming a follower of Christ, Paul invested his life in reaching the Gentiles (non-Jews) with the gospel message and then teaching them how to live a life pleasing to God. Entrusted with a precious message, Paul knew he had to pass it on in order for future generations to experience the joy of knowing God personally. Just as Jesus had selected 12 men to take his message to the world after his crucifixion, so Paul appointed men like Timothy to serve as pastors of key congregations.

During Paul's second missionary journey he visited Lystra where he met young Timothy and asked him to join them on the journey.[7] During their travels, Paul mentored Timothy in Christian leadership. Then after three years of ministry together in Ephesus, Paul developed enough confidence in Timothy that he left him there to pastor the church and to "stop those whose teaching is contrary to the truth" while he traveled on to Macedonia.[8] Paul sent encouragement and instruction to Timothy through the letters we now call 1 & 2 Timothy.

Paul penned 2 Timothy from a Roman jail cell while facing his impending death. These were likely Paul's last words to his dear friend. Yet even in those dire circumstances, his concern was for Timothy and others who would continue spreading the gospel message after he was gone. His final instructions centered on the message and encouraged Timothy in four ways:[9]

Guard the message: "…carefully guard the precious truth that has been entrusted to you."[10] Paul warned Timothy to watch for false teachers who sought to distort the truth of the gospel message.

Study the message: "All Scripture is inspired by God and is useful to teach us what is true and to make us realize what is wrong in our lives. It corrects us when we are wrong and teaches us to do what is right."[11] Paul reminded Timothy that studying the Scriptures would keep him attuned to God's wisdom about how to live life well.

Suffer for the message: "You know how much persecution and suffering I have endured…Yes, and everyone who wants to live a godly life in Christ Jesus will suffer persecution."[12] Paul told Timothy to expect to suffer through difficult times and persecution for the sake of Christ's message.

Spread the message: "You have heard me teach things that have been confirmed by many reliable witnesses. Now teach these truths to other trustworthy people who will be able to pass them on to others."[13] Paul implored Timothy to stay focused on spreading the message through this multiplication strategy. Because men like Paul and Timothy committed themselves to telling others about Jesus, the gospel message continues to thrive today.

Just as Paul composed this letter with important wisdom he wanted Timothy to remember, so Coach Yow also left her most important thoughts for us to consider. A year prior to her death, Coach Yow recorded a video to be played at her funeral in which she shared with family, friends, colleagues and fans the wisdom she gained through her 66 years on earth. She boiled her whole life down to one message: the importance of a personal relationship with Jesus Christ. She could have reminisced about her accomplishments or her great memories of Wolfpack women's basketball, but all she wanted people to remember was how they could know God. And this was the legacy she most wanted to leave–one in which many would find faith in Christ as the most meaningful part of life and would continue to pass his gospel message on to others.

4

Back to the Basics

Lorraine Owen Watson
NC State Wolfpack, 1975-1979

WOLFPACK HISTORY

The first time I met Coach Yow, her passion immediately captured my attention. To her, coaching basketball was not a job, but a passion–truly her life's calling. As a player, I watched her live out this passion day after day. Many practices lasted four hours because of Coach Yow's famous words, "Just one more time." Whether practicing a drill, a play or foul shots, our team joked about what that phrase actually meant, as it usually took 10 to 15 iterations of it before we were really finished! Coach Yow's passion would settle for nothing less than excellence.

Although I came to NC State with a drive of my own, my experiences and time with Coach Yow taught me the necessity of consistent hard work in striving for the best possible outcome. Whether we won or lost, Coach Yow analyzed our performance to determine what we did well and how we could improve. Oftentimes, her evaluation led us back to working on the fundamentals. She firmly believed and taught that we would never achieve greatness by skipping steps or forgetting the basics. As with much of what I learned from Coach Yow, I see how this same principle applies to life. I get busy and before long my most important things take a back seat and disturb a healthy balance between work, family and friends. Moments like this require a "post-game analysis" to get back to the basics.

Another basic I learned is the concept of team–that basketball cannot be won or lost by one person. Coach Yow taught us to acknowledge our teammates for a well-set pick, a great defensive play, a strong box-out, a great shot or a perfect pass. We certainly had stand-out individuals, but the foundation of their success was the team.

Coach Yow's passion for the sport never got in the way of her priority to help us win in the classroom. She expected us to get an education and to manage our schedules, attend class and seek help if needed. A few years after my graduation, she established study times to ensure that her players developed the discipline and habits needed to succeed off the court.

The principles and discipline I learned from Coach Yow have served me well over the years. Now as a software engineer, I recognize that the skills I learned through playing basketball have been just as important as my education. The lessons learned in Coach Yow's classroom gave me transferrable skills that I take to every new opportunity and that give me the foundation and ability to succeed no matter what comes my way.

WOLFPACK WISDOM

For God loved the world so much that he gave his one and only Son,
so that everyone who believes in him will not perish but have eternal life.
John 3:16

Coaches continually evaluate their teams. Whether after practice or a game, a coaching staff banters daily about performance, personnel or strategy in an effort to improve. With all the moving parts of a team, it's easy to get distracted and off-track, forgetting to keep the main thing the main thing. Like Coach Yow, many coaches and leaders find that keeping a team focused requires constant review and further mastering of the fundamentals. This principle applies to our spiritual lives too.

With, quite literally, a church on every corner in many U.S. cities and a staggering number of denominations, it's easy for well-intended Christ-followers to get caught up in debating differences in baptism, communion or worship styles and to lose focus on the central tenet of Christianity. The "main thing" in Christianity is the gospel message–the death, burial and resurrection of Christ.

Coach Yow revisited the fundamentals in basketball, in life and even in planning her funeral. She wanted every moment of her memorial service–from the hymns sung to the words spoken–to proclaim the gospel message and the importance of knowing God through a relationship with Christ. In the video she recorded especially for her funeral, Coach Yow shared these verses fundamental to the gospel message:

For everyone has sinned; we all fall short of God's glorious standard. *(Romans 3:23)*

Though created to experience fellowship with God, our stubborn self-will causes us to go our own way. This self-will, characterized by an attitude of active rebellion or passive indifference, is what the Bible calls sin.

For the wages of sin is death, but the free gift of God is eternal life through Christ Jesus our Lord. *(Romans 6:23)*

The payment for our transgressions is death, or spiritual separation from God. Though we may think we can pay for our wrongdoings by performing good deeds or giving money to the disadvantaged, those aren't acceptable forms of payment in God's book. Someone must die (be spiritually separated from God) to pay the debt we owe. So God gives us a choice—we can pay that debt ourselves by spending eternity separated from him or we can receive his free gift of eternal life through Christ. Thankfully, what God required he also provided…

But God showed his great love for us by sending Christ to die for us while we were still sinners. *(Romans 5:8)*

This is the great news of the gospel! God's love for us is so long, wide, high and deep that he orchestrated a way to pay the penalty for our sins—through the death of his own Son. It's like a judge sentencing a guilty man with the death penalty and then stepping down off the bench, taking off his robe and serving the sentence himself, letting the criminal go free. God said that the forgiveness of sin requires the shedding of blood, and then he went and satisfied that requirement himself.[14] And finally,

If you confess with your mouth that Jesus is Lord and believe in your heart that God raised him from the dead, you will be saved. *(Romans 10:9)*

Receiving God's free gift by confessing Jesus as Lord and believing that God resurrected him from the dead assures us of eternal life with him in heaven. "I've had many victories in my life," Coach Yow said in the video, "many great victories, many championship victories, gold medal victories. But this [eternal life] is the victory of all victories. You can't even compare it to all the others."[15]

This principal—getting back to the basics—is useful in all areas of life. Yet, as Coach Yow made clear through not only her life, but also her death, it's of the utmost importance to get back to the basics spiritually. For our response to the gospel message holds significance not only in this life, but also in the life to come.

5

Strong and Courageous

June Doby
NC State Wolfpack, 1976-1980

WOLFPACK HISTORY

Like many other college athletes, I ventured away from home my freshman year to start a journey that would impact the rest of my life. Little did I know all the ways that Coach Yow would empower me with tools to face some of life's most challenging obstacles. During my basketball career at NC State, I watched the impact of Coach Yow's powerful leadership, both on and off the court. She taught me about respect—that in order to receive it, I must first give it to others. I saw how her faith in God formed the foundation for her daily life and how she always found the positive in any situation.

Of all that I learned from this amazing woman, it was her fight with breast cancer that had the most profound impact on my life. In August 2006, I too received a diagnosis of this horrible disease and had surgery later that year. Watching Coach Yow fight breast cancer with not only determination, but also a positive attitude gave me hope and an inner peace that I could fight this disease too. She showed me how to gracefully accept all that God has allowed to come into my life—both good and bad. She always said that when we give our lives to God, he looks after us and supplies the strength to face any trial that comes our way. I've experienced this truth first hand. Coach Yow's faith and example inspired me to face the toughest challenge of my life head-on and to live each day with God leading the way.

Watching Coach Yow battle for her life gave me the courage to fight harder to survive this disease. Her life served as a testimony to me that I can live with cancer, not die from it. I am proud to say that Coach Yow was not only my biggest role model, but more importantly, my friend. My respect for her has grown immensely since my playing days and her inspiration motivates me to keep living each day to the fullest.

WOLFPACK WISDOM

This is my command—be strong and courageous! Do not be afraid or discouraged. For the Lord your God is with you wherever you go.

Joshua 1:9

Of all the qualities that impacted June's life, Coach Yow's strength and courage left the biggest impression. Countless others stood with June, amazed at the seemingly endless reservoir of strength and courage Coach Yow displayed day after day, year after year. Coach Yow wasn't white-knuckling it or trying to manufacture these qualities on her own. If they seemed supernatural it's because they were. Like the Old Testament leader, Joshua, she drew them from the Lord.

Joshua walked with Moses for years, watching and learning from his leadership. He lived so faithfully that God chose him to lead the masses of Israelites into the Promised Land after Moses died. Despite his training and preparation, some amount of fear most certainly accompanied this mantle of leadership.

When God repeats himself in the Bible it's a red flag to pay attention. He's saying something important. God's redundant message to Joshua was "be strong and courageous"—words first spoken to him through Moses:

> *Then Moses called for Joshua, and as all Israel watched, he said to him, "Be strong and courageous! For you will lead these people into the land that the Lord swore to their ancestors he would give them. You are the one who will divide it among them as their grants of land. Do not be afraid or discouraged, for the Lord will personally go ahead of you. He will be with you; he will neither fail you nor abandon you." (Deuteronomy 31:7-8)*

God knew that leading the Israelites over the Jordan River and into the Promised Land would challenge Joshua on many levels. His

soldiers would disobey God's instruction, leading to defeat in battle.[16] Enemies would use deceptive tactics against him.[17] Fear and
discouragement would beckon him at every turn. Because God
knew what lay ahead for Joshua, this phrase "be strong and courageous" became a mantra of encouragement straight from God's
heart to Joshua's ears:

> *Be strong and courageous, for you are the one who will*
> *lead these people to possess all the land I swore to their*
> *ancestors I would give them. Be strong and very coura-*
> *geous...This is my command–be strong and courageous!*
> *Do not be afraid or discouraged. For the Lord your God*
> *is with you wherever you go." (Joshua 1:6-7, 9)*

Unfortunately words alone don't magically produce these qualities. Perhaps some can muster up internal strength or courage for a
time, but that well of self-sufficiency eventually runs dry. God directs
Joshua to two constant sources of strength and courage: his Word
and his presence.

> *Be careful to obey all the instructions Moses gave you. Do*
> *not deviate from them, turning either to the right or to the*
> *left. Then you will be successful in everything you do.*
> *Study this Book of Instruction continually. Meditate on it*
> *day and night so you will be sure to obey everything writ-*
> *ten in it. Only then will you prosper and succeed in all*
> *you do. (Joshua 1:7-8)*

God reminds Joshua of the importance of the Scriptures, noting
that studying, meditating on and obeying the Truth would keep
Joshua from veering off the path. This remains true even today.
More than just letters on a page, the words of the Bible are alive and
bursting with power–power to bring perspective, instruction and
encouragement. Power to fill our minds with all that is true, right
and good. Power to provide strength and courage to our inner man
when weakness and fear threaten to overcome us.

Coach Yow's favorite verse was Philippians 4:13–"I can do all things through Christ who strengthens me." Like Joshua, she depended upon the Scriptures as a source of strength and courage. This wasn't just a nice phrase to include with her autograph or to quote in a speech. These words empowered her. She believed them. Jesus Christ could strengthen her to face absolutely anything–even cancer. This verse and many others would buoy her spirit, filling her with so much strength and courage that it constantly overflowed to others.

The second source of Joshua's strength and courage was the certainty of God's presence–God's sure promise to never abandon him. Watching God's faithfulness to Moses over the years helped Joshua develop a solid trust that God would hold true to his word. As Joshua faced battle after battle, reclaiming the Promised Land for the Israelites, God remained with him, instructing him about tactics and encouraging him to replace his fears with trust.

Coach Yow also trusted in God's promise to never leave her side. She knew she wasn't fighting alone, and this breathed strength and courage into her soul. Her constant companion and friend–the One who had a plan and knew what was best for her–was with her to the end.

Just as Joshua took the encouragement he received from God and used it to encourage his troops, so Coach Yow took the strength and courage God gave her and passed it on to everyone possible–her team, her fans, her opponents, and perhaps most importantly, other cancer patients like June.[18]

6

The Corner Pieces

Ronnie Laughlin
NC State Wolfpack, 1977-1980

WOLFPACK HISTORY

Coach Yow made a permanent imprint on my life. No doubt about it. Maybe that's because we both hail from the same hometown of Gibsonville, North Carolina. Growing up, I heard over and over about her coaching feats at Allen Jay High School and Elon College. Or maybe it's because my high school coach, Debbie Yow, reflected her sister Kay's coaching style and demeanor. Or perhaps it's because my coach at Peace College was Nora Lynn Finch, who later became Coach Yow's assistant at NC State. Or maybe it's because after playing a year at Peace, I transferred to NC State and enjoyed the privilege of playing for both Coach Yow *and* Coach Finch. In addition, Coach Yow's youngest sister, Susan, was an NCSU assistant. So that's my claim to fame–I played for all the Yow sisters! I am forever linked to the Yow's, but especially to Coach Kay Yow.

During my days in the Wolfpack uniform I would often think to myself, "How does she keep all those plays in her head?" and "Where do her ideas come from?" At that time I did not understand that becoming exceptional in both basketball and life required desire, dedication and most of all, determination. These behaviors formed the corner pieces of the puzzle of Coach Yow's life.

Not once did I question Coach Yow's desire. It shone through in the tone of her speech during pre-game preparation, in her meticulous scouting of our opponents, in her enthusiasm during practice and in her meetings with each player to discuss our positional responsibilities. At game time, I never wondered if Coach Yow wanted to win.

Coach Yow proved her dedication in every practice. I can still see her out on the court "playing" a position to demonstrate how she wanted us to do it. She could play any position—a feisty post player with sharp elbows posting up strong, a deceptive guard with excellent range or a wing setting brutal screens. She dedicated herself to helping us reach our maximum potential.

At the beginning of each year, we set both team and personal goals. Unbeknownst to me, this piece was central to the puzzle of life. Coach wanted us to win more games each season and to go further in post-season play every year. For that to happen, the entire team had to set specific goals and then embody the qualities she modeled for us: desire, dedication and determination. Everything came together for us in 1980 when we won NC State's first Atlantic Coast Conference tournament title and made it to the national tournament. Coach Yow had molded us into a top 20 team—one forever linked by our desire, dedication and determination to be our very best.

Coach Yow became a corner piece in the puzzle of my life. Many people influence us over the course of our lives, but few make an imprint that lasts a lifetime. Coach Yow did that for me. Watching her exhibit desire, dedication and determination in every aspect of her life inspired me to continue to emulate those qualities in my own life.

WOLFPACK WISDOM

Then Daniel praised the God of heaven. He said, "Praise the name of
God forever and ever, for he has all wisdom and power."
                                                    Daniel 2:19b-20

Even beginner puzzle makers know to start with the corner
pieces. They're easily distinguishable and the whole puzzle is built
around those four starting points. Our lives have corner pieces too,
our most important values from which we build everything else. The
three qualities Ronnie noticed—desire, dedication and determination—represented corner pieces in Coach Yow's life. No matter what
she set her hands to, these qualities always seemed to shine through.
The same could be said of the Biblical prophet, Daniel.

As a young man, Daniel was part of a group of Israelites exiled
to Babylon from Jerusalem by King Nebuchadnezzar, who ordered
that some of the "strong, healthy and good-looking young men"
undergo three years of training in the Babylonian culture and religion.[19] The king hoped to foster conformity in the bright, young
Israelite leaders by requiring small acts of compliance that he hoped
would eventually lead to total assimilation. Rather than being
swayed by this attempted indoctrination to worship the pagan,
Babylonian gods, Daniel showed from the very onset of his captivi-
ty the desire, dedication and determination necessary to follow his
God no matter what.

When the young men in training were given food from the
king's kitchen, "Daniel was determined not to defile himself by eating the food and wine given to them by the king."[20] Most likely
Daniel's refusal stemmed from a belief that the food had been sacri-
ficed to idols. But even in his steely determination, Daniel used wisdom and creativity. Not only did he make his request (to not have
to eat the king's food) known through the correct chain of command, but when initially denied, he sought a compromise by asking
for a 10-day trial period during which he and his three friends would
eat just vegetables and water. After the allotted time, the attendant

could compare their physique to the other young men who had eaten the king's food. God blessed Daniel's determination and at the end of 10 days he and his friends looked healthier and better nourished than the other young men.[21]

Daniel's desire for and faith in God's intervention in his life was crystal clear. At one point, King Nebuchadnezzar became infuriated that the men he called upon to interpret his dream couldn't tell him what it meant, so he ordered that all the "wise men" of Babylon, including Daniel, be executed. Daniel promptly went before the Lord, asking him to reveal the meaning of the king's dream to him so that he would not be killed. And his God showed up, telling him the meaning and saving his life. Not only that, but when the king heard Daniel's interpretation, he fell down before him saying, "Truly, your God is the greatest of gods, the Lord over kings, a revealer of mysteries, for you have been able to reveal this secret."[22] And then he appointed Daniel "ruler over the whole province of Babylon, as well as chief over all his wise men."[23]

Lastly, Daniel's dedication to the Lord earned him favor with Nebuchadnezzar and the two kings after him, both of whom placed Daniel in high positions of leadership within their kingdoms. This caused envy among his co-workers who "began searching for some fault in the way Daniel was handling government affairs, but they couldn't find anything to criticize or condemn. He was faithful, always responsible, and completely trustworthy."[24] So they tried to frame Daniel. Knowing that he faithfully prayed three times a day, they coerced the king to make an irrevocable law that any person who prayed to anyone other than the king would be thrown into the den of lions. Yet the threat of death changed nothing of Daniel's dedication to his God. "When Daniel learned that the law had been signed, he went home and knelt down as usual in his upstairs room, with its windows open toward Jerusalem. He prayed three times a day, just as he had always done, giving thanks to his God."[25]

When the last piece is laid, we see the beautiful picture the puzzle creates. When we look at Daniel and Coach Yow, we see beautiful people who lived to honor their God. And it all started with the corner pieces representing principles they held dear—desire, dedication and determination.

7

Commitment– Just Part of the Deal

Faye Young Miller
NC State Wolfpack, 1976-1978

WOLFPACK HISTORY

My twin sister, Kaye, and I played two years at NC State, serving as co-captains our senior season. We experienced great success on the court, but little did I know how the lessons learned then would benefit me even more later in life–at times when I faced making decisions or taking direction.

My time as a Wolfpack woman taught me the importance of commitment. Though not necessarily spoken, every day was a lesson on how the individual and her commitment would determine the success of our team–both in the short and long term. All of us needed to be committed for any of us to succeed. "The strength of the Wolf is in the Pack" was truly something we believed in and lived by. I never really even thought about it as being a choice, just part of the deal.

In the years since I played for Coach Yow, life moments have happened when I had to make a choice or move in a direction. Many times I base these decisions on my belief that some important things in life, like commitment, are black or white. Coach Yow taught me that I can't be a little bit committed. Nor can I be committed only on certain days. I am either in or out. I am committed or I am not.

This makes some decisions difficult. Seldom is the right answer the easy one or the one which makes me or those around me feel good. At times, my decisions as a mother, wife, coach or colleague cause discomfort or strained relationships. Yet, I've sought to stand firm in what I know to be true about commitment—I'm either in or out. Committed or not. And from this perspective, the decision becomes easy.

When I coached high school basketball in Ithaca, New York, our winters were long, cold and snowy, and our season overlapped with the winter break from school. My players and their families anxiously awaited an opportunity to get out of town over the break, in search of warmer weather. Our play-offs, however, started around the same time as the winter break. I decided that any player who could not commit to attending practice during the break could not dress for the sectional play-off games. This decision was easy for me—one I didn't have to think about. Just part of the deal. My players needed to be in or out. A commitment for all practices except those during winter break was no commitment at all.

The father of one player who planned to leave town during break told me that if his daughter was getting more playing time, they would stay home. My response came easily, as it was based on attitudes I developed about commitment years earlier as a Wolfpack woman. Regardless of her role, each player on a team must have the same commitment. Coach Yow believed this and passed it on to me.

Coach Yow's philosophy—the way she treated her players and ran her program—ultimately created in us a realization that many situations which appear to require a decision, actually don't. Modern culture rarely classifies situations as black or white, insisting instead on shades of grey that seem to provide an easy way out. This mentality releases individuals from the responsibility of following through on commitments. I am grateful that Coach Yow demonstrated consistent strength in her convictions and unwavering resolve. It has empowered me to emulate her during some trying times in my life. Times when I ask myself, "What would Coach Yow have said?"

WOLFPACK WISDOM

We worked early and late, from sunrise to sunset. And half the men were always on guard...During this time, none of us—not I, nor my relatives, nor my servants, nor the guards who were with me—ever took off our clothes. We carried our weapons with us at all times, even when we went for water.

Nehemiah 4:21, 23

When it comes to effective leaders in the Bible, Nehemiah ranks among the best. He embodied a plethora of desirable qualities—one of the most important being his passionate commitment and his ability to inspire that same commitment from others. Coach Yow led by example in this same way, never demanding more of a commitment from her players than she was willing to put forth herself.

Nehemiah was a high official serving King Artaxerxes of Persia when he heard about the state of the walls surrounding his homeland, Jerusalem. Years before, the Babylonians had invaded Judah, destroying the city and taking the captive Jews to Babylon. Although some Jews had returned to Jerusalem, its walls (important for their protection) still lay in ruins. This broke Nehemiah's heart and for months he prayed, waiting for the right time to approach the king for permission to return to Jerusalem to rebuild the wall. Eventually the king gave not only his blessing but also provided Nehemiah with soldiers and horsemen to protect him on the journey, letters to governors to ensure safe travel through their territories and an order for the manager of the king's forest to give him timber for the wall.

Nehemiah arrived to Jerusalem and waited three days before secretly exploring the condition of the wall at night. None of the Jewish leaders knew of his plans to rebuild the wall, and he wanted to take stock of the situation before communicating the plan to them. When he addressed them, it wasn't as a visitor dropping in to wreak havoc on their community. Rather, he identified himself as one of them: "You know very well what trouble *we* are in. Jerusalem lies in ruins, and its gates have been destroyed by fire. Let *us* rebuild the wall of Jerusalem and end this disgrace!"[26] What wisdom. Nehemiah knew the importance of these first words of communication to the Jewish leaders. He didn't want them to misunderstand his motive or heart—to see him as some big shot returning to the city to make a name for himself by rebuilding the wall. So he entered the city with a spirit of humility that caused the Jewish leaders to embrace his plan and to respect his commitment to help restore their city.

Mobilizing the community was a crucial part of Nehemiah's project, and he worked his plan to perfection. Nehemiah 3 takes the reader on a counterclockwise tour of the wall, describing in detail the people assigned to rebuild each gate and section:

> *Then Eliashib the high priest and the other priests start-*
> *ed to rebuild at the Sheep Gate. They dedicated it and set*
> *up its doors, building the wall as far as the Tower of the*
> *Hundred, which they dedicated, and the Tower of*
> *Hananel. People from the town of Jericho worked next to*
> *them, and beyond them was Zaccur son of Imri.*
> *(Nehemiah 3:1-2)*

The unfamiliar names make it difficult reading, yet this chapter illustrates the commitment of each person, family and community to contribute to the rebuilding of the wall and the restoration of their city. Nehemiah inspired the people with a vision that they realized could only be accomplished through teamwork.

Such an important undertaking didn't go unnoticed and opposition quickly surfaced. Leaders from territories surrounding Judah mocked the rebuilding efforts and even threatened to attack Jerusalem in an attempt to throw the reconstruction into confusion. But Nehemiah didn't shrink back or give up and his staunch commitment rubbed off on the rest of the workers. He organized ways to protect the people while continuing to build:

> *When our enemies heard that we knew of their plans and*
> *that God had frustrated them, we all returned to our*
> *work on the wall. But from then on, only half my men*

worked while the other half stood guard with spears, shields, bows, and coats of mail. The leaders stationed themselves behind the people of Judah who were building the wall. The laborers carried on their work with one hand supporting their load and one hand holding a weapon. (Nehemiah 4:15-17)

Remarkably, Nehemiah and the people of Jerusalem rebuilt the city wall in just 52 days, a feat that never could have happened without the impressive, committed leadership Nehemiah provided. Centuries later, Coach Yow exemplified the same leadership qualities with her teams. She led with a humble spirit, treating others better than herself. Her commitment to preparation and teamwork inspired the same from her staff and players, as everyone knew they offered something vital to the team. And her persistent effort to overcome opposition gave the team a living example of what it looked like to never, ever give up. To Coach Yow, this level of commitment wasn't a tough decision. It was just part of the deal.

8

See the Heart

Angela Armstrong
NC State Wolfpack, 1979-1983

WOLFPACK HISTORY

As a high school All-American from little Rocky Mount, North Carolina, basketball was my life. My skills earned me numerous honors and awards, including two state championships. For some reason, I found myself drawn to NC State and decided to try out for the women's basketball team. Yes, back in my day we had to try out!

There in the hot, sweaty gym, Coach Yow watched me play for about an hour. I competed hard with the team and felt camaraderie developing quickly. It seemed so natural to scrimmage with them. Afterward, Coach Yow offered me a scholarship—right there on the spot. How sweet to be given an opportunity to be part of the Wolfpack family!

After Coach Yow and I met and talked, my decision came easily. NC State is a great school with a solid reputation. But that's not why I said "yes." Coach Yow is why I said "yes." Even from that first day, she made me feel like a part of the team—like an important member of a special family.

During the four years that I played at State, Coach Yow was more than my coach—she was my second mom. She believed in me, looking beyond my small, 5-4 stature into my heart and knowing that I could play Division I ball. She trusted me (even as a freshman) to run the team offense and defense on the court. She demanded the best of me (and of my teammates) in both the gym and the classroom.

My junior year, Coach Yow recommended that I look into the ROTC program. She said I possessed a "rare leadership quality" important in military service. I didn't know anything about ROTC in the beginning, but trusted Coach Yow's judgment and it changed the course of my life. For 11 years after graduating from NC State, I served in the U.S. Army, earning rank as a Captain. Stationed in Germany, Washington, D.C. and Hawaii during my tenure, I even competed on the All-Army women's basketball team. I cherish those experiences as well as the opportunity to serve my country and am so thankful that Coach Yow suggested military service to me!

"Thank you" seems too simple, short and insufficient to express the overwhelming gratitude and appreciation in my heart for Coach Yow, the opportunity to play for her and the thrill of being part of the Wolfpack family. Quite simply, I owe my life and career to Coach Yow. Even today, I am who and what I am because of her.

WOLFPACK WISDOM

But the Lord said to Samuel, "Don't judge by his appearance or height, for I have rejected him. The Lord doesn't see things the way you see them. People judge by outward appearance, but the Lord looks at the heart."

1 Samuel 16:7

The familiar sayings ring in our ears: "Don't judge a book by its cover" or "It's what inside that counts." Yet, as humans we tend to rely heavily on what we can see as proof of that which we cannot. What a gift to see past the externals and into the unseen matters of the heart! Coach Yow exercised that gift in Angela's life, instilling her with confidence that affected more than her game—it impacted the course of her life. Samuel played a similar role in David's life.

After King Saul disobeyed the Lord's command regarding the destruction of the Amalekites, the Lord rejected him as king, removed him from the throne and directed his prophet, Samuel, to go to the house of Jesse to find and anoint the next king of Israel. Jesse had eight sons, the youngest of whom was David. You can imagine that with seven older brothers, David endured lots of teasing and probably lost scores of wrestling matches! Surely he grew weary of hearing that he was too young or too small to participate in his brothers' activities. Even his chores indicated his place in the family, as daily he found himself out in the fields watching the sheep and goats—a menial job given to one who couldn't be trusted with much.

Here comes Samuel, looking for the next king of Israel, figuring God would lead him to someone tall, strong and handsome. After all, King Saul was "the most handsome man in Israel—head and shoulders taller than anyone else in the land."[27] When Samuel first saw Jesse's sons, he thought the Lord had chosen the oldest, Eliab, who had served in Saul's army and held quite a presence. He *looked* like king material in appearance and height, yet God told Samuel to keep looking. Jesse paraded seven sons before Samuel, but God chose none of them.

Finally, they sent for David to come in from the fields. It seems that they labeled him not just *youngest*, but *least*, *excluded*, and *forgotten*. Perhaps shepherding was always left to the youngest, or maybe David's family relegated him to the fields because they didn't think he could do anything else. Regardless, God created David and knew his heart. And on the basis of what existed *inside* David–his strengths, passions and love for the Lord–God selected him as king.

God specializes in changing the world through people who look common, ordinary or even disadvantaged. He points people to himself by making the impossible and improbable happen through the very people that the world overlooks. It brings him both pleasure and glory to empower the less-than-perfect. Like Angela and David, many of us understand what it feels like to be judged by our cover. *Too short. Too stupid. Too shy. Too slow.* Statements like this can quickly take root in our soul, becoming a self-fulfilling prophecy.

Coach Yow's belief in Angela as a player and a leader provided her with strength and confidence to combat those judgments, excel on the court and lay a foundation for a successful military career. Even if we don't have a Coach Yow in our lives to see past our external limitations and encourage us toward our dreams, we can take heart. We can take courage. Just as God demonstrated his belief in David to lead his people, so God sees our heart and believes in us. And therein lies the ultimate source of confidence, to know that the one true God sees past our exterior into the depths of our heart and loves us with an everlasting love.

9

Humble Strength

Connie Rogers-Newcome
NC State Wolfpack, 1978-1982

WOLFPACK HISTORY

As a high school junior, several top women's basketball programs recruited me. I specifically targeted two basketball camps that summer, hoping to be seriously recruited by one of those schools during my senior year. Coach Yow spoke at my high school spring athletic banquet which excited me, as her camp was one of the two on my list to attend.

Though I followed the Wolfpack women during my high school years, I had limited familiarity with Coach Yow. It took just one week of basketball camp to see the distinct difference between her and the other college coaches I had met. I couldn't put her special demeanor into words. Unlike other camps I attended, NC State's offered chapel services for the campers. Coach Yow often spoke at these gatherings–teaching Bible verses, singing Christian songs and sharing her faith in Jesus. Those expressions of her spiritual life showed her uniqueness. Coupled with her success on the court (the team finished the prior season ranked No. 3 in the national poll), this drew me toward her and created a strong desire to be part of the Wolfpack family. More than anything, I wanted to be part of establishing a tradition of excellence at NC State.

When decision-time came, it was no surprise that I chose NC State as my home for the next four years. Little did I realize how playing under Coach Yow's leadership would mold and shape me. She taught me that the best things in life are free. She always counted her many blessings–priceless gifts like faith, family, friends and health.

Coach Yow taught me that overcoming adversity started with strong belief and reliance on faith in God. During my junior year, my mother was diagnosed with breast cancer. Five hours away from home, I experienced a gamut of emotions. Coach Yow supported me throughout that stormy time, encouraging me to persevere with determination, motivation and inspiration, and challenging me to reach my potential. I learned two powerful scriptures: "When someone has been given much, much will be required in return"[28] and "For I can do everything through Christ, who gives me strength."[29] Both encouraged and inspired me to overcome adversity then, and still do today.

Not one to attract attention to herself, Coach Yow emulated humility and simplicity, yet projected the strength, power and confidence needed to tackle life's toughest challenges. She reminded me of the passage from Billy Graham's book *Life Wisdom:* "God measures people by the small dimensions of humility and not by the bigness of their achievements or the size of their capabilities. God has given us two hands, one to receive with and the other to give with." Coach Yow received God's challenge to touch the lives of student-athletes, and invested her life in teaching, inspiring, motivating and giving to thousands of people, all while demonstrating her love for the Lord.

Thirty years later, I reflect on those four years playing for Coach Yow and am amazed at all the life lessons she taught me—ones that reach far beyond basketball fundamentals. To this day, I carry these life lessons into my professional career as a successful executive account sales and marketing manager. Coach Yow not only molded my character, but left her imprint in my heart forever. Her positive outlook on life, ability to see the potential in others and commitment to develop lasting relationships solidified her legacy with her teams and university, as well as her community, state and country.

Thank you, Coach Yow, for sharing your special gifts with me. I take a part of you with me every day. Your presence graciously blessed my life.

WOLFPACK WISDOM

Humble yourselves before the Lord, and he will lift you up in honor.
James 4:10

Humility is a lost quality in the sports world today. From high school to the pros, nary an athletic event goes by without chest pounding, trash talking or some kind of altercation motivated by an arrogant, in-your-face, I'm-better-than-you attitude. In the sports culture of the day, humble athletes and coaches like Coach Yow stand out like bright shining stars on a cloudless night.

Some think humility plus sports equals soft, weak and powerless. Like athletes or coaches who walk humbly somehow lose their competitive edge. But true humility is anything but weak. Jesus often talked about the power garnered in taking a humble position. Our greatest example taught us humility through not only his words, but also his life, as Paul describes in his letter to the Philippians:

> *Though he was God, he did not think of equality with God as something to cling to. Instead, he gave up his divine privileges; he took the humble position of a slave and was born as a human being. When he appeared in human form, he humbled himself in obedience to God and died a criminal's death on a cross.*
>
> *Therefore, God elevated him to the place of highest honor and gave him the name above all other names, that at the name of Jesus every knee should bow, in heaven and on earth and under the earth, and every tongue confess that Jesus Christ is Lord, to the glory of God the Father. (Philippians 2:6-11)*

These verses remind us that Jesus Christ, the One powerful enough to create absolutely everything, chose to leave the limitless power of heaven to be born in the confines of a human body.[30] But he didn't stop there–he humbled himself further. Though completely innocent, he suffocated to death hanging on a cross for no other reason than to deliver salvation to humanity. God the Father didn't force these events on Jesus. Jesus chose them. He could have bailed, and in the Garden of Gethsemane he wanted to. Three times Jesus asked the Father to take the cup of death away from him, yet in the end he acquiesced to the Father's will over his own, powerfully demonstrating love of others over love of self in the ultimate sacrifice. Truly, "There is no greater love than to lay down one's life for one's friends."[31]

According to Webster's, humility means "freedom from pride or arrogance; lowliness of mind; a modest estimate of one's worth."[32] The irony here is that Jesus was God. A "modest estimate of [his] worth" was exponentially higher than that of any other living being. Yet he *chose* humility, making it all the more remarkable. And because he chose it, God the Father elevated him to the place of highest honor.

What an example. Humility is a choice. When we think of ourselves modestly and put others first, God will lift us up. Coach Yow consistently chose humility. "I still can't believe that it makes a difference to people…the battle that I'm going through," she once said. "I was just trying to do what the Lord was giving me strength to do, and not just to quit living life, but to live it more than I've ever lived it."[33] That humble attitude opened the door for God to lift her up to places of honor in the world's eyes—over 700 wins, an Olympic gold medal, many hall of fame inductions. More important than her basketball success, however, is the place of honor and reverence Coach Yow still holds in the hearts of her players, fans, peers and virtually anyone who ever met her. Honor readily bestowed because Coach Yow walked with such humility.

10

Firm Foundation

Sherry Lawson Ingram
NC State Wolfpack, 1979-1983

WOLFPACK HISTORY

My first memory of Coach Yow took place inside a small rock gym at Allen Jay High School in High Point, North Carolina. My sister, Debbie, played for Coach Yow's varsity team from 1964 to 1968. Only four or five, I tagged along and played on the wooden bleachers while they practiced. I still remember the sweet, musky, leathery smell that hung in the air. That old rock gym represented the first stepping stone to Coach Yow's legendary career at NC State. It still stands today, firm and strong in its foundation. Just like Coach Yow's legacy.

As long as I can remember, I wanted to play for Coach Yow at NC State. I told my high school coaches to throw away any other recruiting letters that came my senior year. I didn't want to read one single letter unless it was from Coach Yow. Attending her summer camps my junior and senior years only reinforced what I already knew. I dreamed of one day donning a Wolfpack uniform.

Though I won the camp MVP award both years, it didn't satisfy. I had my eye on a different award–the distinguished Coach's Award–because that one, it seemed, came from Coach Yow's heart. The winner possessed the qualities she valued most: heart, desire and teamwork. I never won that honor, and later would discover all the reasons why.

My hard work in the gym paid off when I received the tremendous gift of a full scholarship to NC State. All my dreams came true that day! I learned from my high school coaches that I had received over thirty letters from other schools (a lot in that day), but none of that mattered. I was going to play for the greatest coach I had ever known.

Like many freshman athletes, I entered college thinking that my smooth skills would mystify my new coaches and teammates. Instead, I quickly realized that my high school stardom was a thing of the past. I worked my way into the rotation, getting decent minutes each game, yet frustration set in. I wanted more. When I signed my name on the dotted line just a few months earlier, I envisioned becoming the starting star, not getting just 15 minutes a game and a warm seat on the bench. This selfish perspective led me to take action I later regretted.

Still disgruntled with my role on the team, that summer I called another college coach to ask for a transfer. Within minutes of our conversation, she called Coach Yow who, in turn, called my mom. Before I knew it, I found myself sitting nervously in Coach Yow's office on what suddenly felt like the hottest day of the summer. That day began my journey to understanding the true meaning behind the Coach's Award I had coveted the summer before.

I felt humbled before she uttered a single word. Her face showed both disappointment and disbelief. She had entrusted me with the opportunity of a lifetime, and I sabotaged it with just one phone call. It devastated me that I had hurt her. I don't remember the exact words spoken that day, and although Coach Yow stood steadfast, she responded with patience and forgiveness. She continued to believe in me and offered me the tools I needed to reach my potential as both a person and an athlete. I learned, though, that the change had to begin with me.

Coach Yow challenged me to change my attitude, constantly reminding me to think positive even in the midst of defeat. Rather than whine about an obstacle, she taught me to stand up and attack it. "A certain amount of opposition is a help, not a hindrance," she would often say. "Kites rise against the wind, not with it." Slowly, my mindset began to change. I read *The Power of Positive Thinking* by Norman Vincent Peale over and over until I knew it from memory. I worked harder in practice, relishing opportunities to guard Trudi, Ginger and Connie, knowing that they would make me better. I trained harder in the off-season and played with passion and heart, not allowing myself to get down when others continued to start before me.

The team began to take precedence over my selfish desires. I learned to expect little and give much and experienced the rewards of the basic essentials of teamwork–discipline, commitment, confidence and respect for others and self. Finally, I understood what the Coach's Award represented! This transformation not only made me a better player and teammate (I started my junior and senior years), but more importantly, it prepared me for life.

After college, I coached Westchester Academy to two state titles. Pushing my players to be their best, I often found myself repeating Coach Yow's wisdom about teamwork. Now, as the mother of an aspiring basketball player, Coach Yow's influence continues to touch my life. When Meghan was born, Coach Yow sent her an honorary scholarship to play at NC State. Then, when she played on her first middle school team, Coach Yow sat in the stands.

Great coaches care about more than their athlete's performance on the court. Their concern transcends the athlete and embraces the whole person. Coach Yow showed genuine love for Wolfpack players long after their athletic careers ceased. She sent birthday and Christmas cards, she called prospective employers, she remained present. For these reasons and so many more, Coach Yow earned my respect and admiration. She was my friend, my role model, my hero.

From the moment God placed her in my life in that old rock gym over 40 years ago, Coach Yow was a strong, foundational element of my life. I am a better person for knowing her and honored to have played for the greatest basketball coach and most influential teacher of my life–Coach Kay Yow.

WOLFPACK WISDOM

Anyone who listens to my teaching and follows it is wise, like a person who builds a house on solid rock. Though the rain comes in torrents and the floodwaters rise and the winds beat against that house, it won't collapse because it is built on bedrock. But anyone who hears my teaching and doesn't obey it is foolish, like a person who builds a house on sand. When the rains and floods come and the winds beat against that house, it will collapse with a mighty crash.

Matthew 7:24-27

Like Sherry, we're all searching for some solid footing–something sure to build our lives upon. Some choose a career, others a relationship, still others a bank account balance. These foundations, we soon learn, aren't crack proof. Recessions happen. People drift apart. These foundations falter. Coach Yow wouldn't have wanted anyone to build their life upon hers, for she knew her shortcomings would someday bring them disappointment. Yet her consistent presence in the lives of her players–even years after they stepped off the court–provided something they could count upon. They always felt welcomed back to the Wolfpack family and cared for with her compassionate, giving heart.

Still, Coach Yow knew of only one foundation worthy of building a life upon: Jesus Christ. She believed that following his teachings would build a life so strong that it would withstand the even the strongest of storms–a belief based on Jesus' words in Matthew 7 in which he compared two people: one who listened to his teachings and obeyed them, and one who listened but did not obey.

He likened the first to a man who builds a house on a rock foundation–one that won't move, crack or shift. Listening and obeying Jesus' teachings is like being a contractor who pours a foundation correctly and makes sure it's set before building upon it. Even years after that foundation settles, the house stands because its foundation was laid properly. Similarly, when we build our life upon Jesus' trustworthy words, absolutely nothing can move us. The storms of life *will* come, blowing wind, rain and hail against us, but our house—our life, our faith—will stand strong.

Listening to Jesus' instructions but not allowing them to change how we live is like the second man who built his house on sand. Think about that a moment...building a house *on sand*. Most could barely get a house of cards to stand on sand, let alone one of brick and mortar. But that's what life is like for millions of people who attend church and hear the teachings of Christ, but fail to apply those principles to their lives. When dark clouds come rolling overhead, their house—their life, their faith—begins to shake and tremble because it lacks a solid foundation.

When Coach Yow's cancer came back again and again, many watched in amazement at the strength she displayed. She didn't muster this up on her own. Many cancer patients with a more robust physique don't stand with the measure of strength that Coach Yow showed. This supernatural power came from a choice she made years earlier to listen to and obey Jesus' teachings. Year after year she listened and obeyed his words and year after year he proved himself faithful. This process poured a super strong foundation that no obstacle, no storm could crumble. She knew, without an ounce of doubt, that she could trust God with her future, no matter what it held. "At this point I just know that God could heal me at any time, if he chose to do that," Coach Yow stated. "If that was in his will and his plan for me, he would do it. But if he doesn't do it, it's not his plan. And he knows what's best...I can never forget that. No matter what I'm thinking, he knows best, and I have to trust in that."[34] Now *that's* a firm foundation.

11

Peace in Adversity

Claudia Kreicker Dozier
NC State Wolfpack, 1980-1984

WOLFPACK HISTORY

It was my senior year, 1984. We just suffered a heartbreaking, over-time loss to No. 4 Old Dominion on their home court. A win would have put us in the Elite Eight. Instead, our season was over. I struggled to take my uniform off after the game, as it reminded me that our class had failed to bring Coach Yow a NCAA or Atlantic Coast Conference tournament title. I took that failure personally.

As a senior co-captain, I felt like I owed Coach Yow an apology for failing that mission. On the bus ride home the next morning, I fought back tears as I walked to the front. I was surprised to find her peacefully reading a basketball instructional book. I chit-chatted until my heart could bear it no more. Then, through tears and brokenness, I shared my sorrow at failing to help bring her a national title. She looked at me with loving surprise and said, "But Claudia, you gave me so much more than that."

My heart completely melted at her kind words. This was one of the most affirming statements I'd ever received. My heart easily drank it in, and I returned to my seat encouraged. My mind, however, still struggled to accept our failure to bring home a championship title. You can't play in the ACC without becoming fully aware of how coveted a tournament title is for your coach, team and school.

After every practice we huddled and shouted "Wolfpack Women on the way to No. 1 Together!" This was our goal—what we worked daily for years to accomplish. And though we played in the ACC championship game three of my four years, we never won it. It seemed like failure to me, so why was her heart so content?

God used my intense emotions and our interaction on the bus to seal in my memory some important lessons. This snapshot of time showed Coach Yow's true character: her humble and teachable spirit, her peace amidst adversity, her love and compassion.

Thomas Carlyle said, "Show me the man you honor, and I will know what kind of man you are." To write about Kay Yow without sharing that she was molded by her love for and relationship with Jesus Christ, is to share only part of the picture. She walked in humility, deferring praise to God and depending on Jesus for wisdom every day.

Though the Old Dominion loss was a hard blow for her, Coach Yow knew how to be gracefully present where she was, even though it wasn't where she longed to be. Obviously, she would have preferred a win. But she didn't get depressed or beat herself up over the loss. Rather, she sat peacefully reading an instructional book that would help build her coaching skills for the next year. Her peace allowed her to accept her present situation so she could move forward.

I saw this quality in her throughout her life, even as she fought cancer. During one visit I noticed her peaceful heart. Was she where she wanted to be? No! Did she do everything she could to battle wisely? Yes! And yet she walked in peace throughout the process, enjoying her many blessings. Coach Yow didn't defer joy and peace until some great goal or honor was achieved. She had it every day.

Her compassionate response to me on the bus represented a sweet sample of many kindhearted interactions I had with her over the years. I learned valuable lessons from Coach Yow, but the greatest wisdom I gained was to know that her love and friendship were more precious than any championship or honor the world could ever give.

WOLFPACK WISDOM

Don't worry about anything; instead, pray about everything. Tell God what you need, and thank him for all he has done. Then you will experience God's peace, which exceeds anything we can understand. His peace will guard your hearts and minds as you live in Christ Jesus.
                                                                    Philippians 4:6-7

Coach Yow's peacefulness after a tough loss made a strong impression on Claudia's heart and mind. In a world all too familiar with coaches tossing chairs or spewing curse words in response to losing, Coach Yow's peaceful demeanor certainly stood out. Where did she find that calming peace?

Our world believes peace comes from garnering more resources like money or possessions. We're barraged by messages that the high-paying job, shiny new car or dream house are essential stops on the pathway to peace. Buying into these messages may bring peace temporarily, but eventually the emptiness and discontentment returns. Many get stuck in a cycle of more stuff, brief peace, emptiness, more stuff, brief peace...you get the picture.

The world hopes for and works for peace—yet neither hope nor hard work ensures the presence of peace. The world deems peace as the absence of trouble, but in times laden with wars, political/religious conflict and natural disasters, peace seems elusive and impossible to achieve. Growing up, we believe the world's ideas about peace and become disillusioned when the little glimpses of peace we do get, slip through our fingers. Coach Yow taught us, however, that authentic, lasting peace—the kind that quenches our deepest thirst—comes from God, not from the world.

God's peace isn't generated from money or possessions but from relationships, and most importantly, from our relationship with him. In Romans 5:1 Paul states, "Therefore, since we have been made right in God's sight by faith, we have peace with God because of what Jesus Christ our Lord has done for us." Years ago Coach Yow placed her faith in Jesus, believing that his death on the cross provided the payment for her wrongdoings and that his resurrection assured her of eternity in heaven. This act of faith gave her access to his peace. The Jews call it *Shalom*, meaning wholeness, completeness or security—a place of rest for the human soul.

This is radically different than the world's peace! Jesus said it himself: "I am leaving you with a gift—peace of mind and heart. And the peace I give is a gift the world cannot give. So don't be troubled or afraid."[35] A peace-filled world begins in my mind and heart—in your mind and heart. When our minds and hearts soak in the gift of God's peace, it overflows to others.

The remarkable nature of God's peace is that it exists *in the midst* of trouble! Jesus knew how easily our hearts become troubled. Car problems, relational conflict, personal sickness—trials and tribulations bombard us nearly every day. Anyone can experience peace when life is good, but God promises peace even in the toughest of times.

God gives us the choice: peace from the world or peace from him. When we realize the difference, it seems like a no-brainer. Yet the world's messages, laced with enticing but empty promises, distract us away from God's enduring peace.

The verses from Philippians 4 teach us two elements of prayer that can help us experience the benefits of God's peace in the same way that Coach Yow did. First, "tell God what you need." Releasing our need to him not only expresses trust that he can do something about it, but also squelches our worry. Second, "thank him for all he has done." Recounting God's blessings serves as a salve to the soul. Remembering his goodness reminds us that he is faithful to work "all things together for the good of those who love him, who have been called according to his purpose."[36]

Prayer ushers in a peace that exceeds our understanding and guards our hearts and minds against worry. Coach Yow's life was a testimony that re-focusing on God through prayer opens the conduit through which his precious peace flows straight from his heart to ours, no matter what our circumstances.

12

A Silver Lining

Jan Rogerson
NC State Wolfpack, 1982-1984

WOLFPACK HISTORY

As a young child I dreamed of playing basketball in a Red and White uniform for the Wolfpack. While practicing in my backyard I could all but hear the wolves howling each time I made a shot.

It was 1980, and my days as a starting, 5-11 high school senior center were rapidly coming to a close. My coach made contact with Coach Yow, and I ventured to Raleigh for a try-out day. Not long after that exciting but nerve-racking day, I received the disappointing news that NC State did not need anyone my size at that time. Coach Yow suggested a junior college and indicated that the team's needs might change in two years. So off I went to Peace College!

The fun times as a Peace Green Giant forward flew by. Prior to my sophomore season's end, I contacted the Wolfpack basketball office knowing it was my last hope. Tears welled in my eyes, my stomach ached and my heart hurt as "not the right size" stifled my childhood dream once again. I returned home for the summer anticipating transferring to NC State anyway. Through prayer, I finally accepted the fact that I would never play organized basketball again. One hot day early that summer, I meandered to the mailbox for my parents, pondering my future on my way. To my surprise I found a letter addressed to me from NC State Athletics. I quickly opened it, my pace quickening as I returned to the house. With indescribable excitement and disbelief I handed the letter to my dad. His reaction confirmed that I wasn't dreaming. The letter offered me a full scholarship to play for the Red and White!

My preparation began. Trusting my past experience as a power forward and center to provide some level of confidence, this bundle of nerves showed up for preseason workouts only to find I was the fourth shortest player on the team. On top of this realization, I learned that because of my size, my mile time goal was set at six minutes, fifteen seconds–the same time as our 5-4 point guard who was ROTC stock and faster than greased lightning. When God gave out speed, I was too slow to get in line! Needless to say, I ran that red track every day, trying to make my time.

The regular season began and though I gave it my all, I realized my days as a starter were over. I was forward/center material in mind, but guard material in body. And guard I did. For the biggest part of my Wolfpack career, I guarded the water cooler at the end of the bench. I treasured every opportunity I got on the court, especially since Coach Yow let me play the small forward position. Every game, as the pep band played and the crowd roared with cheers I pinched myself for a reality check. On senior night, for the first time in my life, I started as the number two guard. (Perhaps my prayers as a young girl dreaming about this moment were not specific enough!) I left the huddle with the sound of "Wolfpack women on the way to No. 1 together" still ringing in my ears, and overwhelming thankfulness filled my heart for the opportunity to join three other senior classmates (only one of whom started regularly), and a junior point guard in the battle against the Virginia Cavaliers. "Together" we excelled just as Coach Yow expected us to, but probably more so than we anticipated.

Though not a superstar or found in the NC State record books, I learned more about myself and life in those two years than I did my entire basketball career. Enduring the nearly four hour practices along with minimal playing time on game days required a big adjustment on my part, and at times proved difficult. But as Coach Yow so aptly demonstrated, "There is a silver lining in every dark cloud if you just look for it." I looked and saw how many young athletes would have given anything to be in my shoes. I looked and saw the numerous opportunities I would have missed, had I not been part of the Wolfpack women. I looked and saw that in both God's game plan and Coach Yow's strategy, I played an important role. With humility and gratitude through the eyes of faith, I looked and saw that prayers are always answered and dreams really do come true.

Wolfpack Wisdom

"Rabbi," his disciples asked him, "why was this man born blind? Was it because of his own sins or his parents' sins?"

"It was not because of his sins or his parents' sins," Jesus answered. "This happened so the power of God could be seen in him."

John 9: 2-3

Sometimes we just want to know why. Why bad things happen to good people. Why good things happen to bad people. Why dreams for good things like marriage, children or health sometimes don't come true. Why sometimes dreams do come true, but not in the way we envisioned. Why God heals some but not others. A normal expression of our humanity exists in the question *Why?*

In Jesus' time, people thought that a child's physical ailments were caused by his parent's sins. Similarly, we sometimes think our misfortunes result from our misbehavior. Somehow we must deserve the harsh realities of illness, bankruptcy or accidental fatalities. At times the circumstances of our lives *are* the result of our choices. But not always. Innocent men go to jail. Fitness aficionados have heart attacks. Women get breast cancer. In the randomness of life, things happen for which we have no explanation.

Jesus' response to the disciples gives big-picture perspective to their *Why?* question. His answer still holds true more than two thousand years later. Sometimes our challenges are for God's glory. Sometimes our hardships are so others will notice his power.

The apostle Paul understood this. He penned a letter about joy to the church in Philippi–from a prison cell in Rome. "And I want you to know, my dear brothers and sisters," Paul wrote, "that everything that has happened to me here has helped to spread the Good News."[37] He watched first-hand as God used his imprisonment to benefit others. The palace guard heard about Jesus because of Paul's presence. The believers in Rome gained confidence from watching Paul rejoice while in jail, and as a result became fearless in speaking out about God. Though the cloud of his circumstance was dark, Paul saw the silver lining of God's presence, work and power.

Some ask, *Why Coach Yow? Why did this woman who positively influenced so many have to battle cancer again and again?* Perhaps he allowed Coach Yow to experience cancer precisely *because* of her position of influence. He knew when people commented on the strength, dignity and perseverance with which she faced her pain and suffering, she would credit the power of God in her.

Coach Yow saw the silver lining in her fight with cancer. "Maybe it [cancer] is the greatest blessing of all," she once said. "God is using this battle that I might impact other people for him...This is what he has chosen for me and it's good with me because I know that he wants what is best for me."[38]

At first glance, we don't see prison, cancer or the host of life's other challenges as blessings. And yet, those who choose to put their lives in God's hands discover that pain and tragedy offer the greatest opportunity to magnify his power.

13

The Surrogate Mother

Trena Trice-Hill
NC State Wolfpack, 1983-1987
Assistant Coach, 2004-2009

WOLFPACK HISTORY

When I came to NC State in the fall of 1983, the excitement of the men's basketball National Championship still lingered in the air. Parties popped up everywhere! I met students from all over the country and felt fortunate for the opportunity to attend college and start a new life with the Wolfpack family. This home-away-from-home included special people that taught me valuable lessons throughout my collegiate career.

In 1984, I began my second semester at NCSU. I finally felt adjusted to life as a student-athlete and the long hours of going to class, practice, meetings and mandatory study hall. The road would be easy now. At least, that's what I thought!

I lived in Lee Dorm my freshman year with my cousin/teammate, Carla Hillman. One day while sitting in our room, the phone rang. It was my father calling from Virginia. He said, "Are you sitting?" In a panic I answered, "Why?" He started crying, "Your mother died." I immediately dropped the phone and to my knees screaming, "WHHHHHY?"

Carla called Coach Yow and told her what happened. She handed me the phone and Coach Yow said, "Trena, I'm really sorry to hear about your mother. I know she meant a lot to you. She is in a good place now. Heaven is her new home and God is taking care of her. Would you like someone to take you home?" I felt so at ease when I heard Coach Yow's encouraging words..

Coach Yow and her entire staff came to my mother's funeral,

February 16, 1984. At the cemetery, I walked over to Coach Yow and gave her a big hug and thanked her for attending. The following week I was back in school.

Coach Yow taught me that life holds many disappointments like death, illness or tragedy that sometimes lead to feelings of worthlessness or pity. She said, "Don't wallow in self-pity. Swish your feet and get out. God puts us through trials and tribulations so that we can grow spiritually. He doesn't want us to worry about anything. Stay focused on him."

After graduating in 1987, I played professional basketball both internationally and in the WNBA for 14 years. Throughout my basketball career I always kept in touch with Coach Yow. Sometimes I would just call to hear her voice or to simply say, "I love you." She always responded with words of encouragement. She was the teacher, the comforter, the problem solver and the encourager–embracing all her players with open arms and an open heart. To me, she will always be *The Surrogate Mother.*

WOLFPACK WISDOM

Dear brothers and sisters, when troubles come your way, consider it an opportunity for great joy. For you know that when your faith is tested, your endurance has a chance to grow. So let it grow, for when your endurance is fully developed, you will be perfect and complete, needing nothing.
James1:2-4

They say the only sure things in life are death and taxes. Better add troubles to that list. James doesn't say *if* troubles come your way, but *when*. No one in all of history has lived a life free from trials. Financial, relational, medical–we all experience trouble somewhere along the journey. And we can approach them in one of two ways–as obstacles or opportunities. Without question, one of the qualities that made Coach Yow so inspirational was her ability to view every trial as an opportunity. She was a living testimony of the verses above to Trena, and to thousands of others.

At first glance, James' words are puzzling. How can troubles bring opportunities for joy? Should we jump up and down when bankruptcy strikes? Or when our spouse wants a divorce? Should Trena have responded with joy when her mother suddenly passed away?

While we tend to equate joy with happiness (the emotion we feel when we experience something great), the joy James speaks of is based on internal realities, not external circumstances. This kind of joy becomes possible when a soul embraces faith in Christ and finds in him an anchor securing her inner person. This connection with Christ's unchanging character and presence brings the possibility of joy, not in the circumstance itself but in the opportunity it allows to develop qualities like patience, endurance and perseverance. Qualities that ultimately lead us to maturity.

And so we find the purpose of our troubles. God cares more about our maturity than about giving us a pleasant life, so as Peter tells us, he allows troubles to test our faith:

These trials will show that your faith is genuine. It is being tested as fire tests and purifies gold–though your faith is far more precious than mere gold. So when your faith remains strong through many trials, it will bring you much praise and glory and honor on the day when Jesus Christ is revealed to the whole world. (1 Peter 1:7)

A goldsmith purifies metal like gold with high heat that surfaces impurities. He scrapes those off and repeats this process again and again until no more impurities rise to the top. The goldsmith knows the metal has reached purity when he sees his reflection in it. What a beautiful picture of God's work in our lives! He uses trials to turn up the heat in order to surface and remove character flaws and other impurities. As he repeats this sequence, our endurance grows until we reach maturity and he clearly sees his image in our lives.

Coach Yow understood that joy isn't found in the trial itself, but rather in the resulting growth God produces in our lives. Cancer did not carry joy. It brought inconvenient treatments, painful side effects and listless energy levels. But its byproducts–patience, endurance, perseverance and eventual maturity–these qualities increased because of her cancer. And in that way cancer brought opportunity for joy.

14
Perfect Timing

Carla Hillman Yarborough
N.C. State Wolfpack, 1983-1987

WOLFPACK HISTORY

One day during practice in Reynolds Coliseum, we were running a play that required the shooting guard to pop out on the wing and the point guard (me), to "zip" her the pass. The defense intercepted pass after pass as I struggled with the timing. The ball needed to arrive immediately when my teammate reached her spot, and I kept waiting too long. Coach Yow said, "She's only open a split second so you've got to hit her then, otherwise the defense will be there." She repeated herself again and again as my turnovers piled up. I wanted to pass when I felt ready, but that obviously wasn't working. Finally I tried it her way and it worked! That day I learned that the road to success sometimes requires getting me out of my way. It's not about doing things when I feel like it, but rather when the timing is right. As they say, timing is everything.

Coach Yow also taught me about attention to the little things. She said it often–"Pay attention to detail." She implored us to not be satisfied with scratching the surface and to not take anything for granted. One game we trailed Georgia at the half. We had a history of beating them and Coach Yow was extremely upset, not so much about the score as about our lack-luster performance. We simply ignored the details and took our opponent for granted. At half-time in the locker room Coach Yow ranted and raved–in her way, which was pretty mild–and got her message across. In the second half, we took care of the details and came back to win the game. I never forgot that half-time and over the years I've used that phrase many times, especially with my own children.

Coach Yow deeply cared for the well-being of others and how she could assist or bless them. I observed this quality in her since my freshman year and it made her one of the people I most admired.

WOLFPACK WISDOM

Who knows if perhaps you were made queen for just such a time as this?

Esther 4:14b

In team sports, timing can be the difference between winning and losing. Watching teams with impeccable timing is like listening to a symphony. Just as each instrument played at the correct time contributes to the beauty of a symphonic score, so each athlete moving fluidly within the bigger scope of the team creates visual beauty. Through repetition and practice, players develop an innate sense of time and space where they anticipate one another's movements, creating a visual symphony of teamwork. Teams with that kind of chemistry increase their chances for victory and so Coach Yow insisted again and again that Carla get the timing right on her pass.

Although God lives outside the confines of time as we know it, he orchestrates happenings in our lives and in the world that display his perfect timing. From our vantage point, sometimes his timing doesn't seem perfect or even good, but part of walking in relationship with God is learning to trust his timing, even when it appears off. God is weaving together a masterful story throughout the earth—one in which he positions people and circumstances for maximum impact at just the right time.

One of the most well-known Bible verses regarding God's timing is in the book of Esther, which tells the story of a young, Jewish maiden who God moved into the position of queen in order to save her people from destruction. The Bible comes alive in Esther, a book filled with the drama, suspense and heroism of a modern-day movie.

As a young girl, Esther lived in Susa with her cousin, Mordecai, who had raised her since her parents' death. When Queen Vashti refused to present herself to her husband, King Xerxes, he banished her from the throne and after a few years conducted a search for a new queen. Along with hundreds of other girls a lovely, beautiful, teenaged Esther joined the king's harem where she underwent 12 months of beauty treatments before appearing before him. Mordecai wisely instructed Esther not to reveal her nationality or family background—both of which could have disqualified her from consideration. One night with the king was all it took for her to win his favor:

> *The king loved Esther more than any of the other young women. He was so delighted with her that he set the royal crown on her head and declared her queen instead of Vashti. (Esther 2:17)*

Alongside Esther's journey to the throne, a storyline of Holocaust-like evil emerged. In Esther 3 we learn that Mordecai who worked at the king's gate, enraged Haman, the king's highest official, by not bowing down to him. In retaliation, Haman cunningly convinced King Xerxes to issue a decree "that all Jews—young and old, including women and children—must be killed, slaughtered, and annihilated on a single day." Mordecai and the Jews throughout the land mourned at the news and sent a message pleading with Queen Esther "to go to the king to beg for mercy and plead for her people." In those days anyone, including the queen, who appeared before the king without an invitation could be killed. Queen Esther hadn't been summoned by King Xerxes in a month and feared an unwelcomed visit would result in her death. When she communicated this to Mordecai, he responded:

> *Don't think for a moment that because you're in the palace you will escape when all other Jews are killed. If you keep quiet at a time like this, deliverance and relief for the Jews will arise from some other place, but you and your relatives will die. Who knows if perhaps you were made queen for just such a time as this? (Esther 4:13-14)*

Apparently these words struck a chord in Esther, jolting her to see how all the providential steps to her unlikely throne had been carefully orchestrated by God for a purpose beyond royal food and spa treatments. Armed with courage and a plan, Queen Esther approached the king...and lived! In the days that followed, she exposed Haman's evil plot and incited a reversal of fate which found

Haman executed, Mordecai named the king's top advisor and the issuance of a new decree that saved the Jews. Far more than a case of being in the right place at the right time, the intricacies of Esther's story show the hand of a mighty, sovereign God who carefully placed her in the position as queen in order to fulfill a high calling.

Looking back on Coach Yow's life, we see a woman who started out as a librarian and ended up as one of the greatest basketball coaches to ever pace the sidelines. To the untrained eye this might seem like happenstance or sheer luck, but to those familiar with God's providential ways, his fingerprints clearly mark each step of her journey. Coach Yow lived at a time when women's basketball needed pioneers–people who would take the vision of what the sport could become and invest their heart and soul in seeing it happen. People strong enough to fight through the discrimination and discouragement with a spirit that exuded hope, confidence and positivity. People who would simply never give up. In God's providence, Coach Yow was just the right coach at just the right time.

15

Ceaseless Faith

Lisa Speas
NC State Wolfpack, 1985-1986
Graduate Assistant Coach

Wolfpack History

In 1985, Coach Yow brought me into the Wolfpack basketball family as a graduate assistant coach while I completed my master's degree. Prior to arriving at NC State, I had followed her career and felt awed by the opportunity to work alongside her.

First impressions last, and the first thing I noticed about Coach Yow was her intensity. It never stopped, and it rubbed off on those of us around her! Yet, even in those intense moments, she always slowed down enough to ask us "What do you think?" before making her final decision. She probably knew her course of action before asking, but it meant a lot to be included in her processing and many times our answers confirmed the decision she already felt led to make.

Coach Yow's faith in God never ceased. Above all the others, this quality in her impacted me the most. Though I embraced a personal faith in God prior to meeting Coach Yow, her devotion to Christ and life of faith inspired me to become a more deeply spiritual person. Christ served as her constant source both as a coach and as a person fighting cancer.

Over the years, she used basketball as a tool to help hundreds of young women and men learn about and experience God in their lives. Time spent with her caused even those who never believed in God to question his existence. Christ radiated through her, touching those in her presence. After I graduated from NCSU, Coach Yow was chosen as the head coach of the 1988 Olympic team and made a lasting impression on the world when she took Bibles to Koreans who had never known religious freedom.

Shortly before winning gold in the Olympics, Coach Yow was diagnosed with breast cancer. She adopted Jimmy Valvano's "Never Give Up!" motto and lived those words every day of her decades-long battle against cancer. Her intensity, faith in God and never-quit attitude always inspired her teams, the NC State Wolfpack family and countless others.

WOLFPACK WISDOM

Faith is the confidence that what we hope for will actually happen; it gives us assurance about things we cannot see.

Hebrews 11:1

We all have faith in something. We sit in a chair, believing it will hold us up. We board an airplane, placing faith in the pilots and machinery to take us safely to our destination. We tend to think the power rests in the amount of our faith, yet Jesus said it only takes faith the size of a mustard seed (one of the smallest seeds that exists) to move mountains. The power rests not in the size of our faith but in its object. Though I may believe with all my heart that the chair with one broken leg will hold me up, no amount of faith will change the fact that I'll end up on my rear when I sit down. The object of my faith–the broken chair–is not trustworthy.

In the land of many options (otherwise known as America), we're inundated with the opportunity to choose. Whether restaurants, clothes, cars or virtually anything else–we're sure to find a brand or style that suits us. Similarly, modern society offers us many possible gods–Allah, Buddha, money, fame, sex–all vie for our allegiance. But the overriding criteria to inform our decision must be the trustworthiness and power of the person or thing in which we place our faith. And that's how Jesus differs from every other god available to mankind. His love and power–proven ultimately through the empty grave–are unmatched. Through the ages, this God has revealed himself worthy of our faith.

The eleventh chapter of Hebrews, sometimes called the Hall of Faith, reads like a travelogue through the Old Testament, highlighting the journeys of men and women who believed and obeyed God in dramatic and life-changing ways. None lived perfectly, but their strong belief that God would hold true to his promises marked their lives. Take Noah, for example. We're told that "Noah was a righteous man, the only blameless person living on earth at the time, and he walked in close fellowship with God."[39] At that point in history, no one had ever seen a flood, so imagine Noah's confusion when God told him to build an ark. Yet, despite what he couldn't see or understand, Noah believed God, having walked closely enough with him to be certain of his trustworthiness. "Noah did everything exactly as God had commanded him,"[40] and as the waters rose and everything God said would happen did happen, Noah's faith grew stronger.

Or look at Abraham. Talk about trusting in that which you can't see! First God called him to leave home for another land, and Abraham went "without knowing where he was going."[41] Then God told him he'd be the father of many nations, but waited until Abraham and his wife, Sarah, were more than 90 years old before providing their only son, Isaac. After all those years of waiting, wondering and even doubting at times, their faith strengthened as they watched God fulfill yet another promise in his way and his time. But the ultimate test of Abraham's faith came when God told him to sacrifice Isaac–the only one through whom God's promise to make Abraham the father of many nations could be fulfilled. Can you imagine? Yet, Abraham's faith won out over his emotions. He trusted God's instruction over his own logic. And he obeyed, having Isaac at knife point before God intervened and provided a ram for the sacrifice instead.

Many of us struggle with that kind of faith. We want to see, touch and understand before we trust. But like these Hall of Faith saints, Coach Yow had the gift of faith. Believing God came as naturally to her as calling an out-of-bounds play. "I know he loves us with a love that's infinite," she said. "I know he wants the best for us. And I never question why I have cancer. I have no idea, but I know that God has a plan for me. And I just trust his plan."[42] Coach Yow's intimate relationship with God cultivated her confidence that he knew best, even when she couldn't see or understand his ways. She didn't need to know *why* in order to trust him.

Believing God isn't an attempt to manipulate him to get what we want. Coach Yow's faith wasn't dependent on God healing her from cancer. In fact, on many occasions she reflected that whether or not God healed her, she would still trust his plan. In the same way, many of the saints listed in Hebrews 11 didn't receive what they hoped for in this life, but "placed their hope in a better life after the resurrection."[43] They, like Coach Yow, knew that the ultimate goal of even the smallest amount of faith in the one true God was eternity with him in heaven.

16
Intelligent Ignorance

Kerri Hobbs Gatling
NC State Wolfpack, 1986-1990

WOLFPACK HISTORY

My college days as a Wolfpack woman played a major role in shaping me into who I am today. Though my parents provided me with a strong foundation, many exceptional teachers, pastors, coaches and professors positively impacted my life. Among them stands Coach Yow, who served as more of a life coach than a basketball coach. When I think of Coach Yow, many of her familiar sayings come to mind: *When life hands you lemons, make lemonade–When life kicks you, let it kick you forward–Don't wallow in self pity, swish your feet and get out–Attitude is everything.*

There's another, however, that stood out to me then and even today influences my daily life: *Use intelligent ignorance.* Upon first glance, these two words–*intelligent* and *ignorance*–don't seem to work together. How can someone operate intelligently, if he is ignorant?

Intelligent ignorance happens when we focus our mind on a goal and prohibit the thoughts and opinions of others from impeding us. In other words, to exhibit intelligence can sometimes mean remaining ignorant of others' opinions and turning a deaf ear to people who tell us we can't reach our goals because we are women, African American, from a single parent home, a single parent ourselves, from low socioeconomic status or a host of other labels.

Coach Yow taught me how this applied on the court. We played some games where on paper it appeared that an opponent had our team beat. Maybe they had bigger post players who rebounded better than ours, or perhaps their point guard averaged more assists than ours. With *intelligent ignorance*, I learned that many aspects of the game aren't captured on the stat sheet. *Intelligent ignorance* takes into account game-changing intangibles like work ethic and attitude, and literally ignores any consideration of losing.

Coach Yow taught me that practicing *intelligent ignorance* brings freedom to live without the limitations that others may place on me. It allows me to approach situations with an open mind and gives me the freedom to ignore naysayers. I find that even now as a wife, mother and professional, operating in *intelligent ignorance* helps me to achieve great things.

WOLFPACK WISDOM

*Obviously, I'm not trying to win the approval of people, but of God. If
pleasing people were my goal, I would not be Christ's servant.*
                                                    Galatians 1:10

If it's true that sports performance is 10% physical and 90% mental, then the athlete who masters the concept of intelligent ignorance holds an edge over her competitors. Teams that learn to tune out the chatter of media, opponents and even family in order to focus solely on the goal at hand, develop strong unity from their single-minded purpose and oftentimes outperform the opposition.

Intelligent ignorance plays an important part in the Christ-follower's life as well. In ignorance she dismisses the dissenting voices (either the ones in her head or from others) and in intelligence she embraces God's affirming voice (words from Scripture or from people who affirm the truth about her). In essence, intelligent ignorance to the Christ-follower means becoming a God-pleaser, not a man-pleaser.

We'll always encounter doubt. Sometimes it comes from within–that little voice telling us we're not smart enough, thin enough, *you-fill-in-the-blank* enough to reach our goals. And other times it barrages us from the outside–from media, peers, parents or siblings. With all these voices swirling around in our heads, it takes focus and determination to hone in and hear the One voice that matters most.

Throughout Moses' quest to lead the Israelites from their life of slavery in Egypt to the Promised Land, he encountered lots of voices. When God instructed him to go to Pharaoh as the first step in leading the people to freedom, Moses protested–"Who am I to lead the people of Israel out of Egypt?"[44] And later, "O Lord, I'm not very good with words. I never have been, and I'm not now, even though you have spoken to me. I get tongue-tied, and my words get tangled."[45]

Verses like these that show the humanity of saints like Moses bring reassurance by reminding us that the men and women of the Bible experienced moments of doubt just like we do. Moses didn't understand why God chose him for this mighty task. Because he lacked confidence in his leadership and speaking abilities, he pleaded with God to send someone else. Yet God met every doubt with truth and the assurance of his presence:

> *Who makes a person's mouth? Who decides whether people speak or do not speak, hear or do not hear, see or do not see? Is it not I, the Lord? Now go! I will be with you as you speak, and I will instruct you in what to say. (Exodus 4:11-12)*

So Moses followed the Lord's lead, but the voices didn't stop. Can you relate? Just when we finally overcome our self-doubt and start to believe, we're attacked from elsewhere. For Moses, the dissenting voices came from the grumbling Israelites. After many plagues and finally the Passover, Pharaoh allowed the Israelites to leave Egypt only to change his mind and come after them in the wilderness:

> *As Pharaoh approached, the people of Israel looked up and panicked when they saw the Egyptians overtaking them. They cried out to the Lord, and they said to Moses, "Why did you bring us out here to die in the wilderness? Weren't there enough graves for us in Egypt? What have you done to us? Why did you make us leave Egypt? Didn't we tell you this would happen while we were still in Egypt? We said, 'Leave us alone! Let us be slaves to the Egyptians. It's better to be a slave in Egypt than a corpse in the wilderness!'"(Exodus 14:10-12)*

Time and again, the Israelites bombarded Moses with words of disapproval about his leadership and their circumstances. And each time, Moses had a choice about which voices to listen to–God's or the people's. Would he be a God-pleaser or a man-pleaser? Would he use intelligent ignorance or allow all the voices to drag him down and away from God's purposes? More often than not, God's voice took precedence, drowning out the Israelites' complaints, rebellion and personal attacks, and eventually the Israelites made it to the Promised Land.

Like Moses, Coach Yow was a God-pleaser. In running both her program and her life she cared more about God's opinion than man's. As a leader, using intelligent ignorance meant she learned how to ignore any opinions and comments that kept her from fulfilling her calling to serve God through coaching basketball.

Sandra Kay Yow with her parents, Lib and Hilton Yow. (all family photos courtesy of Ronnie Yow)

Yow wore #14, a number her sister, Susan, also wore when she played for Yow at NC State.

Coach Yow coached at Elon College from 1971-75 before taking the job at NC State. (News & Observer)

Coach Yow with her nephew, Jason.

The Yow sisters: Susan, Kay and Debbie

Guiding the Wolfpack women to a 21-3 record in the 1976-77 season. (News & Observer)

Coach Yow led the USA Women's Basketball team to a gold medal at the 1988 Olympics in Seoul, Korea.
(Ronnie Yow)

Coach Yow celebrates her 500th win with her players in Reynolds Coliseum on January 15, 1996.
(News & Observer)

Two legendary coaches: John Wooden and Kay Yow.

Headed to the Final Four in March 1998.

(News & Observer)

Coach Yow directing her team at the 2002 ACC Tournament. (News & Observer)

The 2002 "Tar Heel of the Year."
(News & Observer)

Coach Yow huddles with her team to pray.
(News & Observer)

Coach Yow learned to play basketball here in the backyard of her family home in Gibsonville, NC.
(News & Observer)

Coach Yow recorded her 600th win at NC State with a 65-36 victory over Seton Hall at Reynolds Coliseum on December 2, 2004. (Karl DeBlaker)

On September 27, 2002 Coach Yow was inducted into the Naismith Basketball Hall of Fame. Joining in the celebration were nephews Jason, Zac and Dylan along with siblings Susan and Ronnie.

In 2006, Coach Yow created Hoops for Hope, a game designed to give hope for early detection of breast cancer, hope for increased survival and hope for a cure. (Karl DeBlaker)

Coach Yow greets fans at the 2007 Hoops for Hope game. (News & Observer)

The 2008 Hoops for Hope game raised over $40,000 for cancer research, while the 2009 game (just weeks after Coach Yow's death) raised over $90,000. (Karl DeBlaker)

On February 16, 2007 the court in Reynolds Coliseum was named Kay Yow Court after the Wolfpack scored an emotional victory over rival North Carolina. Just weeks earlier, Yow had returned to the sidelines after missing 16 games to focus on her cancer treatments. (Karl DeBlaker)

Coach Yow's nephew Jason and his wife Melissa named their first child Isabelle Kay Yow.

The Yow siblings: Debbie, Kay, Susan and Ronnie.

Yow's last home game also marked her 1,000th game at NC State–December 14, 2008.
(Karl DeBlaker)

Wolfpack players and coaches put roses next to a Yow jersey at her seat on the NC State
bench during a tribute ceremony in Reynolds Coliseum on January 28, 2009 (Karl DeBlaker)

The 2008-09 NC State media guide cover. (Karl DeBlaker)

17

Heads Up

Sharon Manning
NC State Wolfpack, 1987-1991

WOLFPACK HISTORY

I was so nervous! I arrived at NC State as a freshman, away from home and playing in front of crowds ten times larger than those at my high school. Though unusual back then, I played quite a bit in my first year and even began starting midway through the season. True to form for most freshmen, I made a lot of mistakes—particularly in games.

Unfortunately, my game-time mistakes seemed to multiply. After a mistake, I'd run to the other end of the court and proceed to make another one. With every error, my mental focus and confidence deteriorated more and more. One day Coach Yow called me into her office to talk. Rather than benching me, she made some observations. She noticed that every time I made a mistake I dropped my head. That outward expression of my inward frustration would lead to yet another mistake.

She encouraged me to shake off my mistakes and to make it up to the team at the other end. If I committed a turnover, for example, I could make a play on defense to get it back—stop my man from scoring, grab a rebound, take a charge or block a shot. Our talk increased my confidence on the court, but I realized that this lesson applied to every area of my life. Even today, when I make a mistake I'm reminded of what Coach Yow taught me. I've learned not to respond by dropping my head or getting down on myself, but by trying to do something positive to overcome the error. Just as applying this lesson on the court increased my confidence as a player, so it has increased my confidence in life.

Many coaches wouldn't take the time to sit with a young player, teaching her how to respond to mistakes in order to help her stay mentally tough. Some coaches would grow frustrated, bench the player and hope she figured it out on her own. This separated Coach Yow from all the rest. She was one-of-a-kind, consistently exhibiting these rare and remarkable qualities throughout her storied coaching career. Coach Yow cared not just about her players' on-court production, but equally about their lives outside the gym. Basketball served as her tool to teach life lessons that stayed with her players for years to come. I'm living proof.

WOLFPACK WISDOM

Let us then approach the throne of grace with confidence, so that we may receive mercy and find grace to help us in our time of need.

Hebrews 4:16 (NIV)

Some things unite all humanity: we were born and will die; we need love, food and water; we make mistakes. That last one makes us twinge. No matter how much we dislike it, not one person in the history of mankind (other than Jesus Christ himself) can stake claim to living a life of perfection. Some mistakes, like Sharon's turnovers in a basketball game, qualify as mess-ups. Others like pride, jealousy and stealing we call sin.

The word "sin" was an archery term used by the ancient Greeks that literally meant to miss the mark (and not share in the prize). If the archer shot the arrow and missed the bull's-eye, the scorer shouted "sin!" Whether the shot missed by centimeters or missed the target completely–the result was still called sin. The bull's-eye of life is God's perfection. He alone is perfect and completely pure. In life, missing that standard of perfection is what the Bible calls sin.

Like Adam and Eve in the garden, our first response to our mistakes is usually to hide. Children who disobey steer clear of their parents. Adults who err try to elude the boss. In those moments, most of us also avoid God. Our mistakes strip us of confidence, leaving shame in its place. When faced with our own imperfections, where can we find the confidence spoken of in Hebrews 4:16 to approach a perfect God? The preceding verse gives us the answer:

> *So then, since we have a great High Priest who has entered heaven, Jesus the Son of God, let us hold firmly to what we believe. This High Priest of ours understands our weaknesses, for he faced all of the same testings we do, yet he did not sin. (Hebrews 4:14-15)*

The beauty of God's plan of redemption is that Jesus came to earth and experienced life in a human body. He fought the same temptations we face. He understands what it's like for us. Knowing we will "receive mercy and find grace" can fill our burdened hearts with confidence to move toward God when we make a mess of things—a confidence that rests in who he is, not who we are. Knowing that the consequences or discipline we receive will be wrapped in understanding, mercy and grace can give us the strength to turn from our mistakes, move toward him and receive his forgiveness.

God expects that when we experience his understanding, mercy and grace we'll pass it along to others:

> *Since God chose you to be the holy people he loves, you must clothe yourselves with tenderhearted mercy, kindness, humility, gentleness, and patience. Make allowance for each other's faults, and forgive anyone who offends you. Remember, the Lord forgave you, so you must forgive others. Above all, clothe yourselves with love, which binds us all together in perfect harmony. (Colossians 3:12-14)*

Because Coach Yow had received understanding and forgiveness from God for her shortcomings, she could give that same gift to others. "You can't just love people when they're doing just exactly what you want them to do," she once said. "You have to love them all the time."[46] Coach Yow saw Sharon through her mistake-laden performances by responding with understanding, mercy and grace, which helped Sharon to grow in confidence and learn to keep her head up both in basketball and in life.

18

The Gift of Time

Kristina Kuziemski Bowen
NC State Wolfpack, 1989-1993

WOLFPACK HISTORY

In 1990 my identical twin, Jenny, our friend Danyel Parker and I comprised the freshman class for the NC State women's basketball team. We formed such a tight bond, some joked that we were triplets! We had just endured our first pre-season, and were in the thick of a tough ACC schedule. Winning and earning a ranking as one of the country's top teams made it fun, but we faced major adjustments in learning how to navigate the life of a college student athlete: class, travel and less playing time. Definitely a challenge.

As freshmen, we had "cooler-duty"–the responsibility to bring the drink coolers to and from practice. That may not seem like a big deal, but those heavy suckers hurt our hands to carry! One day after practice, we purposely delayed the inevitable. Instead of immediately taking the coolers downstairs, the three of us stayed on the court, grabbed a seat and unwound with a cold cup of lemon-lime Gatorade.

While we rested, Coach Yow came over, we poured her a cold one and she joined us. To this day, I'm not sure why she did. Maybe she sensed that we needed her. Maybe she just had some extra time in her schedule that day. Whatever the reason, that simple action led to moments that I still treasure today.

After practice drinks became a tradition for us that year. Sometimes we sat in the quiet of Reynolds Coliseum, other times we watched the men's basketball team practice. We talked about everything–classes, family, life, you name it. The only thing we didn't talk about? Basketball. Some conversations lasted only fifteen minutes.

Others, an hour. But no matter the topic or the length, I always felt better when we finished.

To Coach Yow, role didn't matter. Freshmen, seniors, role players or All-Americans—all of us belonged to her team, her family. To her, we were people in need, and Coach Yow always made time in her schedule for people.

We all made it through that year, went on to enjoy successful collegiate basketball careers, and most importantly, graduated. Some of my fondest memories are those precious moments sharing stories by the Gatorade coolers—each second, each minute, each hour, better than the last.

Although my days as a Wolfpack player eventually came to an end, Coach Yow never stopped giving me some of her time. A few years after I graduated she attended my wedding in New Jersey. In fifteen years, she never missed sending me a birthday card with a hand written, personalized note. (She did this for all her former players, but I found her thoughtfulness toward me especially impressive since my birthday is in November, right when basketball season starts.)

Coach Yow continued to give her time, not just to me, but to lots of people. In the hectic world we live in, I can't imagine a more precious gift. She taught me that it doesn't take much to help people and to let them know you care. It just takes TIME, and that's something we can all give—a lesson I will never forget.

WOLFPACK WISDOM

One day as Jesus was walking along the shore of the Sea of Galilee, he saw two brothers–Simon, also called Peter, and Andrew–throwing a net into the water, for they fished for a living. Jesus called out to them, "Come, follow me, and I will show you how to fish for people!" And they left their nets at once and followed him.

Matthew 4:18-20

Time–a precious commodity in a 21st century world obsessed with speed, efficiency, microwaves and drive thrus. Yet for as much as we try to get more time, a day will always equal 24 hours. We all get the same amount of time. The difference is in whether we spend it or invest it. And that difference has huge implications on the kind of legacy we leave.

Clearly Coach Yow loved her players and invested significant time in their lives to communicate that love. Absent of ulterior motives, she genuinely cared about them as people, whether they contributed on the court or not. In this sense, she was no respecter of persons–expressing the same love to the walk-on that she did to the All-American. What a stark contrast to a society where people develop relationships based on a "what can you do for me" mentality, dismissing people who can't help them further their own agenda or who lack the right social status. Turns out society hasn't changed much since Jesus' day, when he often endured ridicule for spending time with tax collectors and other outcasts.

Though the masses followed Jesus from town to town to hear him teach or to see the next miracle, he selected 12 men to live more closely to him so as to learn how to "fish for men." In that day, a rabbi chose his disciples–men who would learn from and imitate his every move. Disciples followed so closely, it was said that they followed in the dust of their rabbi.

If a young man wasn't chosen by a rabbi, he typically began working in his father's business. The biblical accounts indicate the disciples Jesus selected worked as fishermen and tax collectors.

These guys weren't the cream of the crop. They hadn't finished at the top of their synagogue class and weren't selected to follow other rabbis. Yet Jesus chose them and spent three years living with them, teaching and equipping them to fulfill their calling.

Can you imagine how it must have felt to be chosen by Jesus? They didn't make the cut with the other rabbi's, but this new Rabbi–the one everyone talked about and wanted to get close to–he chose them! For three years he literally poured his life into theirs as they watched him teach the masses, perform miracles and field questions from the doubters and skeptics. Jesus invested the last years of his earthly existence living among men who the world saw as common and ordinary because he saw their potential to accomplish the extraordinary. And people noticed:

> *When they saw the courage of Peter and John and realized that they were unschooled, ordinary men, they were astonished and they took note that these men had been with Jesus. (Acts 4:13 NIV)*

Similarly, Coach Yow saw the potential in three freshmen and invested time in water-cooler conversations that meant the world to those young, aspiring players. She could have headed for the office to make recruiting calls or to the film room to watch that next game tape. But instead she invested time in ordinary people who she knew had extraordinary potential. And as these Wolfpack women move through life, many onlookers see their brilliance and take note that they had spent time with Coach Yow.

19

A Season to Remember

Jenny Kuziemski Palmateer
NC State Wolfpack, 1989-1993
Assistant Coach, 1999-2009

WOLFPACK HISTORY

The 2006-07 basketball season started out like many others. Our players returned to school in mid-August to prepare for pre-season workouts. Electricity filled the air with both coaches and players happy to be back on campus and eager to begin another season. Our team blended a great mix of experience and youth with six seniors and six freshmen with a sophomore and junior sandwiched in between. We could tell we had the makings of a special season.

Was it ever! The 'Pack finished the season with a stellar 25-10 record. We played four of the top seven ranked teams in the country, garnered a No. 12 ranking in the final USA Today/ESPN Coaches' Poll, won several games that will go down in Wolfpack women's basketball history, made it to the Sweet 16, and to cap it all off the WNBA selected two Wolfpack players in its 2007 draft.

What made the 2006-07 *A Season to Remember*, however, had nothing to do with wins, losses or final rankings. In actuality, the accomplishments above pale in comparison to the real meaning of the season–a life lesson in faith, hope, courage and perseverance.

In November 2006, our beloved Coach Yow was re-diagnosed with breast cancer. For the second time in three years the cancer recurred, this time with a vengeance–having metastasized to her bones and liver. This forced Coach Yow to take a leave of absence from the team to begin chemotherapy treatments. I don't know who was more devastated, Coach Yow or the team. She never missed practices or games, and now we didn't know when or if she would be able to return to the team. Tears flowed freely in the locker room upon hearing the news. That scene is etched in my mind–each player hugging Coach Yow individually before leaving that night. The next morning we left for a Thanksgiving tournament in Arizona, leaving our Coach behind. During her absence we stayed in contact through phone calls and visits, but realized that only one person could fill the void on our team.

November and December flew by and the New Year brought great news. In January, after several rounds of chemotherapy, Coach Yow could return to the hardwood! For the first time in over two months, she entered Reynolds Coliseum to attend practice. Thunderous applause broke out from her players, coaches and support staff–the same kind of applause she would receive every day for the rest of the season. From that point on, nothing could keep Coach Yow away. We knew how hard it was for her to attend practices and games, so her presence alone lifted our spirits high. The team became a reflection of its Coach, wanting to battle for her the way she was battling for us. Suddenly nagging injuries became inconsequential, eventually disappearing. Suddenly the game of basketball held much more meaning.

As a player, Coach Yow taught me that "It's ok to feel sorry for yourself, but don't wallow in self pity; swish your feet and get out." Now I watched her battle cancer without ever asking why or feeling sorry for herself. She displayed such **COURAGE**–ready to take on whatever cancer and chemo could throw at her.

Once, in the locker room before a big game Coach Yow said, "I want you to remember to have great strength and great courage. There can always be a little bit of fear or nervousness, but courage overcomes that. Your desire to win–to be the best you can be– becomes greater than anything you fear. That's courage." At that moment, we sat in pre-game mode, but as always, her advice applied to all of life. Now, she used that very statement to strengthen her resolve in her fight against cancer. Coach Yow's courage inspired our team. It gave us the strength to take on whatever our opponents could throw at us.

When I played, Coach Yow taught us that "Attitude determines your altitude." She must have said it a thousand times. Connecting the two words in the basketball realm proved easy, but seeing the connection through Coach Yow's fight for life proved more powerful than I can describe. I overheard a player ask if she ever got tired with all the chemo and treatments. "Sure I get tired," Coach Yow answered, "but when I get tired, I go out and walk a mile." Her attitude was filled with **HOPE**. She was going to beat this cancer and we were going to beat anyone that stepped onto the court with us.

From Coach Yow we learned that, "You can't control your circumstances, but you can control how you respond to them." The team could have thrown in the towel without Coach Yow. We had a valid excuse for a less-than-successful year and no one would blame us for lacking focus on the court. But we made a different choice. Circumstances would not get the best of this group of young women. They chose to follow Coach Yow's lead–to work harder than ever and to fight. This effort represented the one way the team felt like it could show their support and love for Coach Yow, proving that they too would **PERSEVERE**.

Most importantly, Coach Yow taught us the importance of her **FAITH**. One of her favorite verses was Philippians 4:13, "I can do all things through Christ who strengthens me." She wrote it on every ball, t-shirt and picture she autographed. Her faith represented the most important element of her life and it showed every day in both her words and actions.

Watching Coach Yow battle her cancer taught us that with courage, hope, perseverance and faith we can push ourselves past the limits of whatever we once thought possible. We observed a direct connection between Coach Yow's actions and all the principles she had taught us in the past. We watched her live her words. She walked the talk–one of the most special gifts she ever gave us. For these reasons, the 2006-07 season was, is and will always be *A Season to Remember*!

WOLFPACK WISDOM

What good is it, dear brothers and sisters, if you say you have faith but don't show it by your actions?

James 2:14

The old axiom is so overused and cliché: Actions speak louder than words. Yet, it holds true no matter how many times we've heard it. What we do and how we act always carries a more powerful message than words from our mouths. Our posture, eyes and facial expressions all say something. A tone, shoulder shrug or sigh all communicate a message.

Coach Yow lived this phrase. She had a storehouse of motivational sayings about courage, hope, perseverance and faith that her players heard year after year. But talk is cheap, and so much easier than living a life true to our words. Speaking about courage and living courageously, for instance, are two different things.

The power of a consistent life—one in which actions and words match—is never more evident than when a teacher, coach or parent gives instruction to those in their care. Such a challenging task, some may play the "Do as I say, not as I do" card to shirk the responsibility. But the more one's life consistently reflects her words, the more powerful her influence in the hearts of those she leads. What if when faced with her own adversity, Coach Yow chose to operate out of fear or to just plain give up? The words she'd spoken over the years would have become like hollow, dead seeds with no power of reproducing. Instead, by acting on her words, Coach Yow planted living seeds of hope, courage, perseverance and faith into hearts everywhere—seeds that bore fruit not only in Jenny's life, but in the lives of all who watched.

The apostle Paul implored young believers to imitate him. "Dear brothers and sisters," he wrote to the Philippians, "pattern your lives after mine, and learn from those who follow our example."[47] Similarly, he encouraged his son-in-the-faith turned church leader,

Titus, to "be an example to them by doing good works of every kind. Let everything you do reflect the integrity and seriousness of your teaching."[48] Paul understood that preaching with words simply wasn't enough. People needed to see the truth of Jesus' message lived out in real life.

Many people reject Christ because they say his followers are hypocrites. They see pastors who speak about honesty but get caught lying, or people who claim to love God and their spouses, but succumb to the temptation of an affair. A little hypocrisy exists in all people because, other than Jesus, none are perfect. Yet as Paul stated, striving to be an example of Christ in both word and deed remains a crucial element in showing people searching for truth the difference Christ makes. People would rather see a sermon than hear one any day–like St. Francis of Assisi once said, "Preach the gospel always and when necessary, use words."

Coach Yow's faith formed the bedrock of her life and provided a strong motivation to live out the words she spoke. After all, this wasn't about her reputation, but God's. She wanted her actions to not only match her words, but more importantly, God's Word. This drive to please God with her life and speech became the force that led her toward a consistent life–one where her actions always spoke louder than her words.

20

Battle Tactics

Sarah McLeod Smith
NC State Wolfpack, 1990-1995

WOLFPACK HISTORY

We had a talented team in 1990-91, earning the third seed in the ACC Tournament. We breezed through the first couple of games, and then faced second-seeded Maryland in the semi-finals. Maryland had beaten us twice in the regular season that year, so we prepared for a tough game.

None of the players realized the mental battle waged between the coaches just prior to tip off. While the teams took the court for pre-game warm ups, Coach Weller from Maryland quietly started her superstitious pre-game ritual. She visited each of the four corners of the court and knocked her head three times, bent down and knocked the court three times and then knocked her head again three times. With all the pre-game commotion, few people seemed to notice her behavior and none of the players gave her a second look. As a red-shirted freshman, however, I noticed this ritual from the bench.

As soon as Coach Weller returned to her team, Coach Yow quickly got up and following the same pattern, went to all four corners of the court and crossed out Coach Weller's good luck charm by dragging her foot across the invisible place where Coach Weller had just knocked. Again, few people and no other players seemed to notice this, but Coach Weller certainly did. Immediately the color drained from her face, and from that point forward the game was ours. We went on to beat the Terrapins 82-75, advancing to the finals where we beat Clemson for the ACC Tournament Championship.

I'll never forget Coach Yow's quick-wittedness and sense of humor that day! From that game forward, our Wolfpack teams prepared for Maryland with a different mindset.

WOLFPACK WISDOM

When you hear the priests give one long blast on the rams' horns, have all the people shout as loud as they can. Then the walls of the town will collapse, and the people can charge straight into the town.

Joshua 6: 5

Humans are funny creatures when preparing for battle, whether in sports or in life. The rituals and even superstitions people keep can bring comfort and sharpen their focus on the task at hand. In sports battles, rituals include everything from wearing a certain color or outfit, to eating the same pre-game meal, to touching the "110%" sign on the way out of the locker room. In military battles long ago, God instructed leaders like Joshua and Jehoshaphat to engage in unique battle tactics that tested full-proof in securing victory.

Upon Moses' death, God assigned Joshua the task of leading the Israelites into the Promised Land (Canaan). Once they entered the land, God directed them to conquer city after city in order to take total control of Canaan. Along the way, he ordered some interesting military tactics. Take Jericho, for example:

> *You and your fighting men should march around the town once a day for six days. Seven priests will walk ahead of the Ark, each carrying a ram's horn. On the seventh day you are to march around the town seven times, with the priests blowing the horns. (Joshua 6:3-4)*

Priests marching around a fortified city blowing rams horns and leading the procession of the Ark–not exactly fierce military strategy. Yet perhaps it took something that bizarre for the Israelites to comprehend that they did not control their own destiny, and that when God told them in advance that he would give them victory (as he often did), he was powerful enough to do it all by himself. He chose to use them, but didn't need their strength or military acumen to defeat the enemy. Indeed, once again he proved his all-powerful nature.

The battle plan God gave King Jehoshaphat of Judah seemed equally as curious. After hearing that a vast army was approaching to attack, Jehoshaphat sought God for guidance. His answer came through a prophet who said:

> *Do not be afraid! Don't be discouraged by this mighty army, for the battle is not yours, but God's. Tomorrow, march out against them. You will find them coming up through the ascent of Ziz…But you will not even need to fight. Take your positions; then stand still and watch the Lord's victory. He is with you… (2 Chronicles 20:15b-17a)*

So Jehoshaphat believed God and followed his instructions. As his army marched out to fight,

> *the king appointed singers to walk ahead of the army, singing to the Lord and praising him for his holy splendor…At the very moment they began to sing and give praise, the Lord caused the armies of Ammon, Moab and Mount Seir to start fighting among themselves…So when the army of Judah arrived at the lookout point in the wilderness, all they saw were dead bodies lying on the ground as far as they could see. (2 Chronicles 20:21-22, 24)*

Another unconventional approach to battle! Victory won through singing praise songs to God. Jehoshaphat's army didn't lift a finger and the enemy attacked and annihilated itself. More remarkable than the unique strategies employed was Joshua and Jehoshaphat's resolve to follow them. Through their obedience they confirmed their strong faith and trust in a God they knew would show up.

Coach Yow said many times that cancer was the toughest foe she ever faced. Her battle tactics obviously included treatments prescribed by her doctors, yet her most powerful weapons were prayer and praise. These may seem like strange tactics, but they positioned her to stay positive and to endure all the challenges of cancer with courage, dignity, grace and hope. Through prayer she kept her eyes focused on God rather than her circumstances, and through praise she remembered all the blessings God had bestowed. And these tactics led her to victory–not in the form of beating cancer, but in running an amazing, inspiring race that led her to the ultimate victory…eternity with her God in heaven.

21

Motivational Silence

Kolleen Kreul Newsome
NC State Wolfpack, 1991-1995

WOLFPACK HISTORY

Coach Yow had great respect for John Wooden. At the top of his *Pyramid of Success* rests the solitary block called *Competitive Greatness* defined as "Be at your best when your best is needed" and "Enjoyment of a difficult challenge." Coach Yow exemplified *Competitive Greatness* and taught it to her players. Like the majority of college athletes, I pursued avenues outside my sport after graduation, but the *Competitive Greatness* engrained in me through my experiences as a Wolfpack woman continues to influence my life and career. Whether I'm teaching my child a life lesson or sitting in a job interview, I continually draw from the well of examples, situations and knowledge that I gained from playing for Coach Yow.

Many times I'm not sure she realized that she was teaching us. The most powerful lessons came not from her spoken words, but rather from her actions. Ralph Waldo Emerson once said, "What you do speaks so loud that I cannot hear what you say." Coach Yow lived this! Her actions opened such a clear window into her feelings and state of mind that oftentimes words were simply not necessary.

Thankfully, Coach Yow was not a screaming, get-in-your-face coach. She didn't need to be. She had her own way of motivating, and many times that involved silence. I learned quickly that when she didn't like my last pass or shot, she remained silent. Our team endured many moments of silence after bad plays, short and to-the-point post-game talks or quiet bus trips home from games. But when she loved my last shot or play, I only had to look at the way she clapped her hands to know it.

The most important lesson I learned from watching Coach Yow's actions regarded her relationship with the Lord. She personified the fact that Christianity is not a religion, but a relationship. I am eternally grateful that the Lord led me to NC State, for that is where I started my own personal relationship with him. Who better to serve as my role model than Coach Yow? She learned early on in her career as a coach and mentor that her relationship with God mattered most, and she maintained that priority. Every game or practice during my career ended with prayer.

Many feel blessed by Coach Yow's commitment and dedication to Wolfpack women's basketball and to the university. No program in the country can match the loyalty and respect that Coach Yow maintained throughout her career at NC State. Whether we graduated in 2008 or 30 years ago, the Wolfpack women always felt at home with Coach Yow and her staff when we set foot on campus. The continuity of her presence blessed every member of our Wolfpack family.

Coach Yow's career extended far beyond the wins and losses. A walk through Reynolds Coliseum makes evident her remarkable dedication to the university, program, staff and players. I can only quote Coach Yow herself, not only as a testament to her life, but also as way to live to my own: "I do not know what the future holds, but I know who holds the future."

WOLFPACK WISDOM

Understand this, my dear brothers and sisters: You must all be quick to listen, slow to speak, and slow to get angry.

James 1:19

Basketball can bring great elation and utter frustration nearly within the same moment, like when a player makes a great steal and then misses the fast break layup. The frenetic pace of the game requires quick thinking and decision-making by players and coaches alike. It's a tense environment in which words sometimes slip out the mouth before they run through the brain. Any Wolfpack woman would attest to Coach Yow's intensity and competitiveness, yet she was a "player's coach." Her style didn't include verbal tirades or a quick fuse. Instead, she had mastered the art and the power of silence.

While certainly applicable to human relationships, James 1:19 was meant to help Jesus' followers learn to relate to God. Listen to the truths of the Bible first, James reminded, before speaking your mind or responding in anger. Listening requires hearing more than the spoken words. Real listening seeks understanding. As James penned these words, maybe he remembered the challenges his cohort Peter had in this area. Known for his all-or-nothing manner, Peter often spoke first and listened later.

In Matthew 26 when Jesus predicted that his disciples would abandon him, Peter blurted out, "Even if everyone else deserts you, I will never desert you."[49] Then, when Jesus informed Peter that he would, in fact, desert him before the rooster crowed three times, Peter declared, "Even if I have to die with you, I will never deny you!"[50] Peter didn't understand, refused to listen and eventually reaped the consequences of his quick tongue. After he cut off the ear of a guard who came to arrest Jesus in the Garden of Gethsemane, Peter denied that he knew Jesus three separate times to bystanders in the courtyard. Then, when Peter heard the rooster crow, "Suddenly, Jesus' words flashed through Peter's mind: 'Before the rooster crows, you will deny three times that you even know me.' And [Peter] went away, weeping bitterly."[51]

Listening first and speaking second doesn't come naturally to most of us, even when relating to the God of the universe. It takes focused effort to close the mouth and open the ears, but wise people exhibit this kind of self-control.

For years Coach Yow made listening to God a priority. Even with the busy schedule of a Division I coach she regularly attended a weekly Bible study. Her love for God produced a hunger for his words and a commitment to listening, understanding and obeying them. Perhaps the practice of quickly turning an ear to God aided her in becoming quick to listen to people.

Although Coach Yow used silence as a motivational tool—discerning when her players needed words of instruction, just a look or no response at all—she also practiced silence off the court, consistently making time to listen to people. Whether a coffee-shop cashier, a fan requesting an autograph or a Wolfpack woman, Coach Yow made anyone she ever met feel special and important because she had mastered the art of silence.

22

People Matter

Jennifer Howard Wolgemuth
NC State Wolfpack, 1993-1997

WOLFPACK HISTORY

Growing up playing basketball in North Carolina, I heard about Coach Yow and her strong influence in the world of women's basketball at a young age. I was excited to attend Kay Yow Summer Camp in the early 1990s to finally meet and learn from this Olympic gold medal winning coach.

I had a blast at that first camp, and soon thereafter Coach Yow offered me a scholarship to play for the Wolfpack women. Each summer during the next four years I stayed in Raleigh to play ball, get ahead with my schoolwork and work Coach Yow's camp.

As both a camper and a coach, the most amazing part of basketball camp was always Coach Yow herself. I'd expected a hall of fame coach with her résumé to be like other sports figures that have an "air" about them, always waiting for others to acknowledge their greatness. Not Coach Yow. Her down-to-earth, genuine nature set her apart. She talked to every girl at camp, from the smallest camper barely able to dribble to the all-star recruit. She watched them compete, wanting each one to learn the proper fundamentals. Coach Yow made herself easily accessible to the campers and treated everyone the same.

Even after I graduated, I continued to work Coach Yow's camp. One summer, I was touched when she took the time to talk with me. Several months before camp, my husband and I had miscarried, losing our baby early in my first pregnancy. It was the lowest point of my life thus far. Though I don't remember her specific words, Coach Yow listened to me pour out my feelings and offered encouragement as I talked. It meant so much that although she had many other things to do, she still took time to listen to me share my troubles.

Facing life's challenges oftentimes brings out our truest selves. Coach Yow remained the same whether she was healthy or fighting cancer. While no one would ever choose to have cancer, she embraced it as an opportunity to handle hardship with character and dignity. When I played, she told our team over and over that although life brings many things outside our control, we can always control our attitude and how we respond. She consistently modeled principles like this one, realizing that living out what she taught created the most powerful testimony of all.

Coach Yow's gentleness and humility complemented her passion for life and love for God. While she strove to help her players excel on the court, she preferred they excel in life. She knew that God had gifted her to coach and sought to use that gift to honor him, helping as many young women as possible along the way.

WOLFPACK WISDOM

The woman was surprised, for Jews refuse to have anything to do with Samaritans. She said to Jesus, "You are a Jew, and I am a Samaritan woman. Why are you asking me for a drink?"

John 4:9

Some people exude a welcoming spirit–their warmth wrapping itself around everyone they meet. This was Coach Yow. It didn't seem to matter if she was rubbing shoulders with celebrities at a hall of fame induction or teaching little kids how to dribble at camp–she paid attention to people simply because they were people. And in her wake she left myriads of people, young and old alike, feeling like they mattered to the world.

Jesus had a similar effect on society. He constantly surprised the teachers of the day and even his own disciples by the ways he interacted with people–especially those shunned because of sickness, racism, physical disability or immoral behavior–many of whom were women.

Jesus lived in a male-dominated culture where women were defined by their ability to bear their husband's children and satisfy his sexual needs. Viewed as a temptation that would cause men to sin, women were barred from public life. Their presumed lack of intellectual ability prohibited them from studying the Torah. In a culture where women were largely dismissed, Jesus turned heads by treating them with dignity and respect.

One of Jesus' most stunning interactions with a woman took place by a well in Samaria. John 4:4 indicates that Jesus "**had** to go through Samaria," to get from Judea to Galilee (bold, mine), but most Jews of that day refused to travel through Samaria, usually taking a longer route around its borders just to avoid setting foot on Samaritan soil. They disliked the Samaritans because they had married non-Jews, among other reasons. But rather than go around, Jesus took the direct route and:

Eventually he came to the Samaritan village of

Sychar…Jacob's well was there; and Jesus, tired from the long walk, sat wearily beside the well about noontime. Soon a Samaritan woman came to draw water, and Jesus said to her, "Please give me a drink." He was alone at the time because his disciples had gone into the village to buy some food. The woman was surprised, for Jews refuse to have anything to do with Samaritans. She said to Jesus, "You are a Jew, and I am a Samaritan woman. Why are you asking me for a drink?" (John 4:5-9)

Village women typically visited the well in the early morning hours to avoid the heat, so this woman's noontime trip for water shows an intentional avoidance of the other women, perhaps because her reputation caused gossip and stares. After all, she had been married five times and now lived with a man who wasn't her husband.[52] Yet, the most astonishing part of this scene is that Jesus actually spoke to her—not just a woman, but a Samaritan woman. In a culture that frowned upon conversation between men and women, and at a time when the Jews hated Samaritans, this radical move surprised both the woman and, upon their return, the disciples.[53] Imagine how she felt that this mysterious, Jewish man treated her— the outcast, the ridiculed, the Samaritan—like a person. Like she mattered. And she did, not because she could give him anything or make him look good (for she could do neither) but simply because she was his creation and he loved her.

No one would have questioned Jesus had he chosen to treat this Samaritan woman the same way society did. But instead, his revolutionary ways and radical love caused people to take note of a different way. A way that brought faith to the sick and disabled. A way that brought hope to the outcast and ridiculed. A way that brought love to the thirstiest of human hearts.

This same love motivated Coach Yow. She received unconditional love from God and sought to pass that love on to anyone she met, regardless of their age, race, gender, or status. Jesus gave her a special ability to love people well, and she did so by extending warmth to everyone she met, hoping they would know they mattered not only to her, but more importantly, to God.

23

Between These Lines

Tami O'Connell White
NC State Wolfpack, 1993-1997

WOLFPACK HISTORY

For four years I played for NC State as a walk-on. Every post-season I performed a cost-benefit analysis to determine whether or not to play the following year–and every year I decided YES. The opportunity to learn from Coach Yow always tipped the scale in favor of remaining on the team. Although I could not articulate it at the time, I subconsciously realized that I learned much more about life, leadership and organizational dynamics by playing with the Wolfpack women than from my textbooks or classes. Lessons like *Dip your toes and keep moving* (regarding feeling sorry for yourself) and *You got to WANT it* (internalizing and visualizing goals) come to mind. But one impacted my life more than the rest: *Between these lines.*

Since graduating from NCSU (over 10 years ago), this lesson has reverberated in my mind at least once a week–sometimes even in Coach Yow's voice! Coach Yow reiterated again and again that once we entered these lines (the perimeter of the basketball court) our thoughts must focus solely on basketball. This reminder helped us let go of the daily stresses and focus on what was at hand–whether practice, a game, strength training or conditioning. When between the lines, we couldn't do anything to fix a situation or relationship causing us stress. While she cared deeply about our life situations and concerns, Coach Yow taught us how to avoid carrying them onto the court and allowing them to ruin a practice or game. She encouraged us to apply this principle conversely too. After a game, for example, we could do nothing about a missed free-throw, turnover or loss. She reminded us that mentally replaying our mistakes could negatively affect other areas like sleep, studying or relationships.

Between these lines influences my decision-making even now as I navigate work and life. I think of it when I leave a meeting with thoughts and concerns swirling in my head, but need to prepare for my next meeting or task. And even more importantly, it comes to mind when I need to choose to leave work stress at work and not allow it to distract me during precious time with family and friends. Through this principle, Coach Yow taught me to be present and focused in the moment because life is made of moments! As a result, I've learned to balance family, career, friends, recreation and spirituality by reminding myself to stay *between these lines* in order to make the most of every moment of my life.

WOLFPACK WISDOM

So Peter went over the side of the boat and walked on the water toward Jesus. But when he saw the strong wind and the waves, he was terrified and began to sink. "Save me, Lord!" he shouted.

Matthew 14:29-30

Athletes the world over have found their sport to provide a safe place to experience release from the other demands of life. Stepping between the lines on the field, court or track brings familiar sights, sounds and smells. Skills practiced over and over give a certain rhythm to moments, hours and days, while physical exertion reduces the normal stresses, worries and anxieties of life. Entering the field of play gives athletes permission to focus on their game, yet sometimes distractions sneak in and disrupt that focus. Like most coaches, Coach Yow implored her athletes to learn how to maintain focus in spite of the competing voices vying for their attention.

The interaction between Peter and Jesus in Matthew 14 shows how this concept of focus applies to our spiritual lives as well. On the heels of miraculously feeding over 5,000 men, women and children with just five loaves of bread and two fish, Jesus insisted that the disciples get in their boat and head to the other side of the Sea of Galilee–a body of water known for its quick-rising storms–while he retreated to a solitary place to pray. Sure enough, in the middle of the night, the disciples found themselves tossed about by strong winds and rising waves.

When they first saw Jesus walking to them on the water, they thought he was a ghost, but then he spoke to them: "Don't be afraid," he said. "Take courage, I am here!"[54] True to his speak-first, think-later personality, Peter called to him, "Lord, if it's really you, tell me to come to you, walking on the water."[55] Jesus' affirmation sent Peter over the side of the boat and onto the water. Focused on Jesus, he actually walked on top of water. This wasn't some David Copperfield illusion–the man actually walked on water. Focused. Intent. Trusting.

Then, suddenly the wind and the waves stole his attention from Jesus' face. Maybe a gust blew through his hair or a big wave crashed at his feet. Whatever happened, Peter was distracted by his environment and began to sink. Just a split second snapped his focus and affected his ability to walk where he never had before. Peter's lesson here is echoed in the book of Hebrews when the writer encourages Christ-followers to "...run with endurance the race God has set before us. We do this by keeping our eyes on Jesus..."[56] The marathon of life demands endurance over hills, deserts and swamps and through exhaustion, tired legs and blistered feet. Making it through every season, storm and circumstance to the finish line requires intense focus.

Coach Yow demanded focus from her players and from herself. Her love for basketball and for her players sharpened her ability to focus. And in her last few seasons, stepping between the lines became a lifeline–a motivation to endure the next chemo treatment and a welcome distraction from the physical nausea and pain that threatened to overwhelm her. Yet the number one focus of her life was Jesus himself. "Focus on God," she said, "because then God becomes big and the problem becomes small. But if you focus on the problem, then the problem becomes big and God becomes small."[57]

As the refrain of the famous hymn *Turn Your Eyes Upon Jesus* so simply states:

> *Turn your eyes upon Jesus,*
> *Look full in His wonderful face,*
> *And the things of earth will grow strangely dim,*
> *In the light of His glory and grace.*[58]

With her focus on Jesus, Coach Yow knew that everything between the lines in basketball and in life would fall into its proper place.

24

One Day at a Time

Kenyatta Williams Hankerson
NC State Wolfpack, 1995-1999

WOLFPACK HISTORY

Leaving my hometown in Louisiana and moving to NC State without my family and friends meant facing many unknowns. Would I get along with my roommate? Would I like the food? Would I make a difference on the court? I felt scared and uncertain, but like a mother, Coach Yow took me under her wing.

When I felt afraid or lonely and had no one to talk to, I knew I could turn to her. She became a safe place for me to share my fears and my dreams. She encouraged me to take one day at a time, to spend less energy worrying about tomorrow and to remember that doing my best today would make me better tomorrow. I took those words of wisdom with me to both class and practice every day.

One time I had to speak in front of a large audience for one of my classes. Talk about terrified! Coach Yow helped me tweak my speech and listened to me practice until I had it down. I received a good grade and soon after was asked to speak at a sports banquet. With Coach Yow in my corner, I not only overcame my fear of public speaking but grew to enjoy it.

Though I didn't anticipate a future in basketball after college, Coach Yow coached me like she thought I could continue playing if I wanted to. One day in practice I was trying to out-rebound the tallest player on the team. At 5'5" this was a big challenge for me! I worked hard, but was disappointed when I still didn't get the rebound because it meant our group had to run. Before Coach Yow blew the whistle for us to run, she stopped practice.

"Do you know why I like you so much?" she said. "No," I

answered. "Because you are so competitive," she replied.

That statement has stayed with me even today as I run my own business. Coach Yow taught me that competitiveness and striving to be the best are positive qualities, especially when the odds are against me. On the court it meant not pouting after a turnover, but getting back on defense. In life it works the same way. When things don't go well, rather than sulk I pick my head up, figure out how to prevent it from happening again and make it a better tomorrow.

Coach Yow's role in my life far exceeded that of basketball coach. After all these years I continue to apply lessons she taught me, realizing how her influence has spilled over into every corner of my life.

WOLFPACK WISDOM

So don't worry about tomorrow, for tomorrow will bring its own worries. Today's trouble is enough for today.

Matthew 6:34

As a college freshman, Kenyatta struggled with something that plagues many people: worry. Our jam-packed lives moving at lightning speed leave us at a loss for how to control it all. And those of us brave enough to admit that the "control freak" label might apply, may also agree that the elusiveness of control is at the root of our worry. For as much as we walk through life with fists clenched around that which we seek to control, we soon come to realize a glaring truth: We ultimately possess no control over anything.

We've heard of and perhaps known people who control their eating and exercise in order to prevent disease, only to suffer a heart attack while out for a jog. Or parents who provide a loving, stable home for their children only to have one child choose the high of drugs over the love of his family. Our pursuit of safety and security is threatened nearly every day by things outside of our control. That lack of control fosters worry about everything from our mother's health, to funding our retirement, to the big game this weekend.

Jesus knew the human propensity for worry and need for security, so he purposefully addressed those concerns. In Matthew 6:25-34 Jesus encouraged his followers not to worry about the things of everyday life. His reasoning was simple: Birds never lack for food or flowers for splendor, and God values humans much more than either birds or flowers. Surely if he takes such great care of them, he will take even better care of people. Jesus taught that the antidote for worry is trust in the One powerful enough to control all that which we cannot. This sounds simple–don't worry, just trust God. It may be simple, but it's not easy. Those of us paralyzed by worry can find freedom in the same way that Jesus taught his followers and Coach Yow encouraged Kenyatta–one day at a time.

The Bible applauds the wisdom of planning, but when our concerns for the future steal our joy for today, then we experience the crippling affects of worry. Living in the moment means staying present to this day, this hour and even this minute. It means trusting that God will provide what we need for today, and when tomorrow comes, he'll do it again. The Israelites learned this in the wilderness when God miraculously gave them manna (bread) every morning.[59] He instructed them to take just what they needed for that day and when they did, everyone had enough to eat–everyday. Those who tried to save some for the next day for fear that God wouldn't come through, found manna infested with maggots when they awoke. Day after day, God verified his trustworthiness to his people and even after all these years, he remains the same trustworthy God. *He will come through.*

Coach Yow told Kenyatta that putting her energy into doing her best today meant she would be better tomorrow. Choosing to focus on the present and trusting God with the unknowns of the future takes humility (acknowledging that we don't have control) and faith (believing that God has both control and our best in mind). Humility and faith helped Coach Yow stay present-minded. Even (and especially) in the face of cancer, she embraced the reality that worry could not add a single hour to her life and she chose to find the good in each day.

25

Willing to Sacrifice

Chasity Melvin
NC State Wolfpack, 1994-1998

WOLFPACK HISTORY

Coach Yow represented both coach and role model to me. Every season at NC State brimmed with experiences that taught me a lot about basketball and even more about life. The special memories etched in my mind are literally too many to count. Two that stand out remind me of Coach Yow's essence as both a coach and a person.

When I first visited State, I saw David Thompson's jersey hanging in the rafters at Reynolds Coliseum. I told Coach Yow that I wanted my jersey to be retired one day. She looked at me and said, "You can do it, but it's going to take a lot of hard work." She was so confident, never doubting that I could accomplish whatever I set my mind to. She was right. My successful collegiate and now professional career is the result of faith and hard work. Coach Yow set the example for me through her own faith and hard work. Today, my jersey hangs in the rafters of Reynolds Coliseum, and each time I look up and see *Melvin, #44* I think about taking the risk to share my dreams with a woman who also took a risk and believed that I could achieve them. Everyone has a dream inside, and it takes a special person to coach that dream to reality. Coach Yow was that kind of person to me.

One day during practice, Summer Erb and I were hammering out our post drill workout while Coach Yow watched. As we did our post moves, she used a hitting bag to simulate defense and to provide contact. Just picture Summer and me (6-6 and 6-3, respectively) in our post stance, looming over Coach Yow, hoping we wouldn't hurt her! Neither our size nor our height phased her one bit. She kept encouraging us, all the while pushing us in the back with the bag. Her primary focus and concern (even above her own personal safety) was our development—making us better, more aggressive and more determined. Many coaches would ask an assistant to step in or arrange for practice players to play defense, but memories like this one show the personal attention to detail that made Coach Yow one of the greatest coaches ever.

WOLFPACK WISDOM

Work willingly at whatever you do, as though you were working for the Lord rather than for people. Remember that the Lord will give you an inheritance as your reward, and that the Master you are serving is Christ.
Colossians 3:23-24

Paul wrote these words to encourage Christian slaves in Colossae to obey their earthly masters. He urged them to work sincerely (with pure motives) because of their reverent fear of the Lord–regardless of whether their master was watching or not.[60] Paul reframed work as a higher calling to serve not only men, but more importantly, God. Along the same lines, he reminded the Corinthians how placing their faith in Christ would alter their life focus:

> *Since we believe that Christ died for all, we also believe*
> *that we have all died to our old life. He died for everyone*
> *so that those who receive his new life will no longer live*
> *for themselves. Instead, they will live for Christ, who died*
> *and was raised for them. (2 Corinthians 5:14b-15)*

Jesus' sacrifice is too much for the human mind to comprehend. He endured torture, ridicule and one of the most horrific punishments devised by man–crucifixion. When we believe that Jesus willingly suffered so intensely on our behalf in order to set our hearts free and give us new life, gratefulness wells up from deep within, unearthing a desire to live for his purposes and not our own. This perspective was behind the strong work ethic that Chasity saw in Coach Yow. Life itself became an expression of gratitude for the love, grace and mercy God extended to her through Christ. In addressing the Romans, Paul put it this way:

> *And so, dear brothers and sisters, I plead with you to give*
> *your bodies to God because of all he has done for you. Let*

them be a living and holy sacrifice–the kind he will find
acceptable. This is truly the way to worship him.
(Romans 12:1)

In light of all that God has done for you, Paul pleads, give him your body–your whole self. And in so doing, worship him, ascribing honor to his name. Traditionally we view worship as time spent at church or Bible study. But the kind of radical worship Paul speaks of here flows outside those boundaries and into every moment of our lives. Giving our bodies to God in worship means that no matter where we go or what we do–whether we are coaching, washing dishes or battling disease–our goal is to worship him.

And so Coach Yow offered her body and life as an act of worship to the God who paid the ultimate sacrifice for her. Though she consistently loved and cared for her staff and players, she didn't labor only for them. Though her passion for and loyalty to NC State ran deep, the university wasn't her ultimate boss. The chief end of all Coach Yow's labor was to worship and honor God.

In Christ, she found unconditional love and acceptance that provided intrinsic, consistent motivation. While she enjoyed the victories, honors and awards, she didn't *need* them in order to find validation and worth–she already had those things in her relationship with God. His unconditional love gave her the drive to work hard as an act of service to people and of worship to the Lord, knowing that her ultimate reward existed not in a dusty trophy case, but in her heavenly inheritance.

26

Happily Herself

Summer Erb
NC State Wolfpack, 1996-2000

WOLFPACK HISTORY

I started my college basketball career at Purdue University in 1995. After a season full of ups and downs, the entire coaching staff was released. That sent me and a few of my teammates into a downward spiral, trying to figure out what to do next and what the future would hold. After being released from my scholarship at Purdue, I ventured out to find the right place for me for the *next* four years of my life.

Home is always a good place to start, so I went back to Lakewood, Ohio for the summer and called my high school coach. He told me that NC State had been in constant contact with him. After talking things over with my family, we decided that an official visit to Raleigh might hold something special for me.

The Wolfpack coaching staff knew how heartbroken I was about what had happened in West Lafayette. My family and I sat with them in Case to have an open conversation about NC State and Purdue. Out of nowhere, Coach Yow spoke up. She said, "Summer, I know how you feel about Coach Dunn, and I would never try to replace her. I can only be who I am." At that moment, tears flowed freely in the room. My family and I stepped outside and talked things over for a couple of minutes, but my fate was sealed. I would forever bleed Red and White.

Coach Yow held true to what she told me that day. To me, she became so much more than my coach. She saw me through some hard times, and she was right there for the brilliant times–the Final Four, graduation and my first coaching job.

Infinitely more than just a part of my past, Coach Yow made a difference in my life that will forever color my future. She was and continues to be a mother figure to me. I love you, Coach Yow.

WOLFPACK WISDOM

Then Saul gave David his own armor–a bronze helmet and a coat of mail. David put it on, strapped the sword over it, and took a step or two to see what it was like, for he had never worn such things before. "I can't go in these," he protested to Saul. "I'm not used to them."

1 Samuel 17:38-39

As Summer considered transferring to NC State, Coach Yow emphasized that her goal wasn't to replace Coach Dunn. Coach Yow knew herself and realized the futility of trying to be anyone else. She refused to participate in the comparison game that sometimes leads people to try to become someone they're not.

It's human nature to survey the landscape to see how we stack up against professional colleagues, respected leaders or even our next door neighbor. If we don't like what we see we may try to mimic people we see as successful, only to discover that their strategies don't work for us. Coach Yow learned that her coaching style had to reflect her strengths and personality. David learned a similar lesson as he approached his infamous fight with Goliath.

In times of war, a soldier's family had the responsibility to provide for his needs, so David's father often sent him to take food and supplements to his older brothers who fought in King Saul's army. When David visited his brothers during their battle with the Philistines he heard the champion Philistine warrior, Goliath, scream out threats to the Israelite army. Appalled, David asked the soldiers "Who is this pagan Philistine anyway, that he is allowed to defy the armies of the living God?"[61] When King Saul heard about David's question, he sent for him.

Picture young David, not yet old enough to be a soldier in the Israelite army, telling King Saul that he will go fight the Philistine champion Goliath who stood over nine feet tall! David persisted and eventually Saul consented, even trying to help by giving David his armor to wear. In that day, a king's armor represented his position and wearing it would have put David in rare company, if not in a category all by himself.

Yet David wasn't starry-eyed or swayed by the special treatment. When Saul's armor swallowed him up, David realized he had a better chance in combat if he went with what he knew–stones and a sling. With impressive self-awareness for a teenager, he passed on the royal armor, opting instead for five smooth stones, his shepherd's staff and a sling.

David fought and killed Goliath because he stayed true to himself. Coach Yow found coaching success because she remained true to her core strengths and values. Both found victory because they were brave and mature enough to be themselves.

27

Beacon of Hope

Kristen Gillespie
NC State Wolfpack, 1996-1999
Assistant Coach, 2007-2009

WOLFPACK HISTORY

I will never forget the first time I met Coach Yow on my recruiting visit in the summer of 1995. I could tell instantly that this woman stood for so much more than winning basketball games. From that day forward, I knew with certainty that I wanted to play for this coach and allow her to help guide me through my collegiate experience. During my four years at State I learned so much more than X's and O's. Coach Yow showed me how to live life. She always instilled an incredible sense of confidence in all of us. No matter what the odds, she made us believe we could conquer any obstacle that came our way.

Since leaving State, I've not only faced, but overcome, times of adversity because of the foundation Coach Yow laid for me. I always wondered if others outside the lucky few who donned the Red and White jerseys noticed her steadfast character and enduring faith. Not until I returned to State in 2007 did I see first-hand the far-reaching nature of Coach Yow's influence. In every arena we entered, a sea of pink shirts greeted us in the stands. Opposing players waited for Coach Yow to come out to the court just to shake her hand and speak with her. She received standing ovations from fans at every game when she entered the court and again during team introductions.

Coach Yow's faith and courage spoke to the nation. Witnessing this reception from basketball fans all over the country, I realized that her mission on earth reached far beyond just winning ball games. Coach Yow was a beacon of hope for everyone who faces hardship–pretty much all of us! To God, developing our character holds precedence over giving us pleasant circumstances, and those who endure life's challenges with strong and God-honoring character will experience the ultimate victory. Coach Yow lived with a deep understanding of this truth and God used her to teach it to others. Her example showed me the necessity of seeking God in times of disappointment or despair and of understanding that if I am obedient to his will, I will receive what he's promised me.

I will never forget what I witnessed during our 2007-08 season. Coach Yow taught me that through faith in God, you can overcome anything and be a source of inspiration for those who struggle to believe.

WOLFPACK WISDOM

I pray that God, the source of hope, will fill you completely with joy and peace because you trust in him. Then you will overflow with confident hope through the power of the Holy Spirit.

Romans 15:13

Hope. It's become one of those all-occasion words. I *hope* we win. I *hope* she gets home safely. I *hope* the car starts. We use it in so many different contexts, the true meaning becomes diluted and powerless. Hope in this sense is just as Webster's defines it: "To desire with expectation of obtainment."[62]

But in God's economy, hope represents so much more than this cross-my-fingers kind of desire. For people who place their faith in Christ, hope becomes "confident trust with the expectation of fulfillment"[63] because of their source of hope—the unchanging, all-powerful Jesus Christ. We all want to confidently trust something. If our lives aren't like shifting sand, then they're like a turbulent sea. Something always changes and the unseen future remains just that—unseen. We never know what's around the corner. So this hope that Jesus offers appeals to our easily discouraged hearts, and we're magnetically attracted to people who have it—people like Coach Yow.

Through her relationship with God, Coach Yow experienced hope that anchored her soul, as described in Hebrews 6:18b-20:

> *Therefore, we who have fled to him for refuge can have great confidence as we hold to the hope that lies before us. This hope is a strong and trustworthy anchor for our souls. It leads us through the curtain into God's inner sanctuary. Jesus has already gone in there for us.*

An anchor for the soul—something to keep us from wandering off course or into danger. There's not a person alive who doesn't desire that kind of security. Picture a large ship outside a harbor. It can't navigate its way safely to shore without help from a tugboat.

This small but mighty tugboat attaches itself with rope lines to the vessel and pulls it to shore. This illustrates the kind of sure hope that Jesus offers us. If we're the ship, then Jesus is the tugboat and our destination, heaven, is the harbor. When we receive him by faith, he secures us to himself and pulls us safely to our eternal home.

The verses in Hebrews 6 carry rich symbolism. In the Old Testament Temple, a curtain hid the Holy of Holies–the inner sanctuary–from the people. Only the high priest had permission to enter, and then only once a year, to atone for the people's sins. When Jesus died on the cross, the curtain tore from top to bottom symbolizing that now, anyone who believes in him has open access to God.[64]

These truths gave Coach Yow hope–a confident hope generated from the assurance that no matter what she faced on earth, she would spend eternity with God in heaven. Onlookers often marveled at Coach Yow's joy and peace, as both seemed unlikely companions on a journey through pain and suffering. But those who knew her understood her secret: a heart filled with a confident hope from God. So much hope that it easily overflowed to others, making her a beacon of hope to friends, colleagues and basketball fans everywhere.

28

The Wounded Soul

LySchale Jones
NC State Wolfpack, 1995-1999

WOLFPACK HISTORY

Leaving for college is an exciting but scary experience for most freshmen. Abandoning the comfort of family and friends to enter into new experiences with new people can challenge even the most secure people. For me, it was even tougher because during my senior year in high school, my mother died of breast cancer.

Needless to say, my adjustment to my new family was more than a little rough. Many times I approached people and situations as if the world owed me something. I tended to pout and whine. One day during a preseason workout on the track (my least favorite part of campus) I was trying to get out of running and Coach Yow looked at me and said, "What a baby. It is OK to swish your feet in your problems and pity," she continued, "but you have to get out, you can't soak in it."

It seemed like every workout from that day forward, she would make a hand gesture suggesting that I needed to swish my feet. She continued to call me a baby–"Schale what a baby, baby Schale," she would say. "In fact that's what I am going to call you from now on: Baby Schale." And that has been my nickname ever since.

As if getting a nickname wasn't enough to help me correct my reactions, there was always Reynolds at 6 a.m. Time and time again I'd have to meet Coach Yow at the gym to run, and after each session we would go to Case Dinning Facility for breakfast. During these times Coach Yow mentored me, coached me, guided me and imparted her wisdom to me. Reflecting on these times, I see how Coach Yow mothered me. Her discipline wasn't punishment, but an expression of her love. She wanted to reach me and if I couldn't be reached the easy way she resorted to making me run. After my behavior, I would expect the same from any coach.

Coach Yow didn't stop there, however. She went the extra mile to show me how much she cared. So we shared conversations over breakfast–conversations which now have become powerful life lessons. In her wisdom she saw things that I lacked and ways my foundation needed rebuilding. LySchale's growth as a person was just as important (if not more so) as Baby Schale's growth as a basketball player. Coach Yow always challenged me with quotes during those morning talks. One, "Good is the greatest enemy of excellent" taught me the importance of tapping into my excellence. I had great talent, but would never reach my maximum potential if I grew content with just being good.

During my mom's illness, about ten college coaches came for home visits. Mom's cancer had worsened and she didn't know much about any of the schools. Not wanting to sway my decision, she never said much after the coaches left. But after Coach Yow's visit she said she wanted me to go to the Wolfpack. She saw something in Coach Yow that put her at peace.

My feelings for Coach Yow run so deep, it's hard to put them into words. People often ask me if I wish I would have gone to a different school and I can boldly say "NO." Another coach may have led me to the Final Four more times, but I doubt that any other coach would have made the effort to shape me into a better person the way Coach Yow did. It took time and compassion to see past my anger and walls into my wounded soul. Coach Yow met me right there, saw past my pain and hurt, and through love, led me to a better life.

WOLFPACK WISDOM

No discipline is enjoyable while it is happening–it's painful! But after-ward there will be a peaceful harvest of right living for those who are trained in this way.

Hebrews 12:11

Loving discipline. Many of us wouldn't put those two words in the same sentence, yet they reflect not only Coach Yow's approach with LySchale, but also God's approach with his people. Love is commitment, not emotion. Discipline is training, not punishment. Loving discipline holds people accountable to a standard of excellence in a way that shows care and concern, not degradation or belittlement. No one could blame LySchale for feeling anger when her mom died, yet when she expressed her anger with a rebellious attitude that negatively affected the team, Coach Yow had to address it. *How* she disciplined LySchale set her apart as both a coach and a leader.

It's easy to grow frustrated with people with rebellious attitudes. Many head coaches would not meet players at 6 a.m. at the gym—they'd assign that job to an assistant. Those coaches who do show up at the gym may do so resentfully, communicating their frustration through a tone of voice or body language. This isn't the picture LySchale paints of her interaction with Coach Yow during those early morning workouts. She enforced the consequence for bad behavior by making LySchale run and yet showed a loving commitment to her by taking the time to go to breakfast. The listening and mentoring that happened there tangibly showed LySchale that Coach Yow cared not only about her development as a player, but also as a person. LySchale began to see that this discipline had benefits.

The beauty of Coach Yow's approach rests in how accurately it mirrors God's discipline. God loves us so much that he refuses to allow us to stay the same. When we mess up, he faithfully corrects us, as a shepherd would his sheep. We picture shepherds as meek and mild, and certainly their job requires gentleness, but it also demands toughness. Shepherds carry a rod—a club usually made from a young sapling whittled to just the right size for their hand. The rod protects both the shepherd and the sheep from danger, but also serves to discipline any sheep with a propensity for wandering away on its own. Shepherds throw their rod with great speed and accuracy at either a predator (to protect their flock) or at a sheep (to keep them from wandering into danger). While it may seem unkind to throw a club at a defenseless sheep, this action corrects and protects the sheep, keeping it safely within the flock.

This illustrates God's heart toward us. As Hebrews 12:10 says, "God's discipline is always good for us…." When we wander off the path or behave in ways displeasing to God, his discipline serves to train us, that we might live right lives. As children, we may protest a parent's discipline, yet deep within rests a thankfulness that someone cares enough to enforce boundaries and behavioral expectations. Our hearts eventually respond the same way to God's discipline. His care and concern, even clothed in the form of discipline, brings the comfort expressed in Psalm 23:4b—"Your rod and your staff protect and comfort me."

Although LySchale surely grew weary of 6 a.m. workouts, underneath the surface she felt thankful that Coach Yow took time to care for her heart in the midst of a flood of pain. And in the end, discipline brought comfort and healing for LySchale's wounded soul and led her on a path toward a better life.

29

Fake It 'til You Feel It

Tynesha Lewis
NC State Wolfpack, 1997-2001

WOLFPACK HISTORY

Coming off freshman-of-the-year honors and an almost 17 points-per-game average my sophomore season, I had high expectations for this, my junior year. But the junior jinx started early when during preseason workouts I lost all love for the game. I decided that I didn't want to play basketball and felt completely burned out. I called my mom and dad and explained that I'd had enough. I was tired of practicing. I was tired of weight training. Even the mention of the word basketball made me tired. My dad said I didn't have to play anymore and that he supported whatever decision I made. Since he could afford to send me to school without my scholarship, I was done with practice, done with coaches and done with anything related to basketball.

I finally got the nerve to call a meeting with Coach Yow. When I walked into the office and sat down, Coach Yow looked over her desk and said "What's up, T?" I told her I was tired, burned out and that I didn't want to play basketball anymore. Though I felt totally frustrated with the situation and my lack of desire to play ball, I sat there looking around at all the pictures on the wall and said, "I just can't do this anymore." I shared about my dad's support and willingness to pay for my education if I lost my scholarship.

I awaited her response and anticipated a Bible verse, because that is one thing Coach Yow and I always agreed on: Jesus. Instead, she responded with a request. She said, "T, sometimes you have to fake it 'til you feel it." I looked around to be sure that it was Coach Yow talking. I laughed. "Are you serious?" I said.

"Today in practice I want you to do this for me," she continued. "I want you to be excited and cheer for everything that happens and then tell me how you feel at the end of practice."

Now, although I thought this was the craziest thing Coach Yow had ever asked me to do, I would have run through a wall for her, so I agreed. That evening I got to practice and did exactly what she said. When my teammate threw a bad pass, I said, "good bad pass" and then got all excited about the next play. My teammates dribbled down the court while I screamed and cheered up and down the side-line. They thought I had bumped my head! But by the end of practice I had fallen back in love with my first boyfriend–basketball.

"Fake it 'til you feel it." I am so grateful for that lesson and for a coach of Coach Yow's caliber and intelligence. If I had quit like I intended I would have missed out on exciting junior and senior campaigns, not to mention six years of professional basketball. I feel blessed to have experienced those four years in Coach Yow's presence and to call myself a Wolfpack woman. "Fake it 'til you feel it" has kept me in a lot a places when I thought about giving up, only to find out that my promotion or blessing was just a cheer away.

WOLFPACK WISDOM

Rejoice in the Lord always. I will say it again: Rejoice!
                                        Philippians 4:4 (NIV)

When life presents challenges, it's tough to ignore how we feel. Our gut tells us to make decisions based on those feelings, even if it means disregarding previously made commitments. We don't *feel* love anymore, so we want to divorce. We don't *feel* like making good on the business contract, so we want to renege. We don't *feel* like finishing the season, so we want to quit. Problem is, our feelings are unpredictable at best–like crazy weather that brings rain, snow and sunshine all in the same day–making them a poor barometer when it comes to producing good decisions.

Acknowledging the unreliability of our feelings can help us better navigate our journey and make sound decisions. Realizing beforehand that we may wake up some days not feeling love for our spouse, for example, may give us the perspective needed to prevent an impulsive reaction. Paul offers another strategy to help at times when our feelings don't match our commitments–he recommends a healthy dose of rejoicing. This was Coach Yow's advice to Tynesha and it helped pulled her out of a tired, burned-out state of mind.

In the above verse, "rejoice" means to be cheerful. In Paul's short letter to the Philippians, he used this word seven times. Remarkable, considering all he'd endured for the cause of Christ:

> *Five different times the Jewish leaders gave me thirty-nine lashes. Three times I was beaten with rods. Once I was stoned. Three times I was shipwrecked. Once I spent a whole night and a day adrift at sea. I have traveled on many long journeys. I have faced danger from rivers and from robbers. I have faced danger from my own people, the Jews, as well as from the Gentiles. I have faced danger in the cities, in the deserts, and on the seas. And I have faced danger from men who claim to be believers but are not. I have worked hard and long, enduring many sleep-*

less nights. I have been hungry and thirsty and have often gone without food. I have shivered in the cold, without enough clothing to keep me warm. (2 Corinthians 11:24-27)

Exhausting! He must have experienced feelings of burn-out and frustration along the way, wanting nothing more than to give up and go home. A lot less adversity would send many folks packing. Instead, Paul put into practice the wisdom he regularly proclaimed to others—rejoice and be cheerful in the Lord. When circumstances threaten to discourage and depress, think about God's goodness. Look at the bigger picture. Find joy in the free gift of salvation. In essence, direct your attention to God rather than to the situation. Paul learned that choosing to rejoice in God during tough times provided perspective and strength for another day, a principle Coach Yow also learned and lived by long before her cancer reoccurred.

Bombarded with adversity in one form or another nearly every day, many college coaches grow weary of the constant challenges and find it hard to keep fighting. Yet throughout her career, Coach Yow's trademark was her positive attitude. She rejoiced in God by recounting his blessings, even in the face of a lost game or another chemo treatment. This resulted in a glass-half-full kind of life.

Coach Yow wanted Tynesha to grasp a similar lesson—that choosing to rejoice in the joy of playing basketball in spite of her feelings could rekindle her love for the game. Coach Yow could have quoted a verse, like Tynesha expected. Or she could have come down on Tynesha for wanting to back out on her commitment to the team. Instead, she applied timeless wisdom from the Bible to help Tynesha experience the life-changing power of rejoicing in all things.

30

Bury the Bad

Talisha Scates
NC State Wolfpack, 1998-2002

WOLFPACK HISTORY

I fell in love with Coach Yow's coaching spirit long before I came to NC State. I entered school in the fall of 1998–just after the Wolfpack women played in the Final Four the previous March. I watched their semi-final game with anticipation and remember the determined look on every coach and player's face. Even via television, I got a taste of what I would experience as a member of the Wolfpack family. That moment inspired me and my future teammates to strive for another trip to the Final Four–not just to experience it ourselves, but more importantly, to help Coach Yow get there again.

Coach Yow was known for her inspirational quotes. We always looked forward to hearing what new quote she had for us. One of my favorites was: "It's okay to have butterflies (referring to emotions before a game) just as long as they are flying in formation." Coach Yow continually found new ways to inspire and motivate us. She recognized that each team had a different mix of people and personalities that oftentimes brought unique challenges. Such was the case my junior year.

After a horrible first half of the season, Coach Yow instructed the team to meet upstairs on the practice court. We figured that meant she planned to run us hard, just like in pre-season. Instead, she told us to sit down and gave us a piece of paper on which we were to list all the negative things that happened during our season so far. Each person folded her paper and put it into a box. Coach Yow picked up the box and we followed her outside where she had dug a hole in the ground in front of Reynolds Coliseum. That's where we buried all of those bad things. This exercise was so simple, but it made a huge impact on us. We had a phenomenal second half of the season and made it all the way to the Sweet Sixteen.

I learned so much from my experience at NCSU and from Coach Yow. Even today people ask me if Coach Yow was as wonderful and genuine as she seemed from afar. Whether from a distance or up close, Coach Yow was the classiest, most genuine, authentic person I've ever known.

WOLFPACK WISDOM

I don't mean to say that I have already achieved these things or that I have already reached perfection...No, dear brothers and sisters, I have not achieved it, but I focus on this one thing: Forgetting the past and looking forward to what lies ahead, I press on to reach the end of the race and receive the heavenly prize for which God, through Christ Jesus, is calling us.

Philippians 3:12-14

One of the greatest challenges of coaching is the mystery of motivating athletes. Some respond to "get on the line" and others don't. Some need to be spoken to calmly, others instructed with a more, well...passionate tone. Individuals form a team and things become even more complex. Every coach feels the weight of figuring out how to motivate both the individuals and the team toward its goals. Even though college teams usually add just a few new players each year, the slightest change in personnel creates a completely different dynamic and requires new motivational techniques. As a result, what worked last year probably won't work this year. Coach Yow accumulated quite an arsenal of motivational tactics in her 30-plus years on the sideline. The one she used with Talisha's team mirrored a principle Paul wrote about related to spiritual growth.

Paul wrote to the Christians whom he had visited twice in Philippi, encouraging them to rejoice in all circumstances, pressing on to finish the race. In the first part of Philippians 3, Paul expressed how his earthly qualifications and accomplishments paled in comparison to knowing Christ. When compared to Christ, he called all earthly gain garbage—literally dung. Paul longed to know Christ with every cell of his being, yet realized that he had not attained perfection (meaning completeness or maturity). He still had some miles to cover.

Paul's strategy to finish the race was to focus on just one thing. Even in those simpler days without television and texting, distractions existed. So Paul sought to narrow his concentration to one thing to give himself the best chance of finishing the race. Today, college athletes live in a world flooded with distractions. Coach Yow often reminded her players that stepping on the court provided a unique opportunity to leave everything else behind and to focus on that one thing–basketball. With everyone focused, the likelihood of the team reaching its goals increased dramatically.

Paul concentrated on one thing: "forgetting the past and looking forward." In this instance "forget" doesn't mean "fail to remember" but rather "no longer influenced or affected by."[65] Paul wasn't suggesting that he could magically erase the mistakes of his past and literally forget them. Rather, he understood that to know Christ more meant breaking the power of the past by living for the future.[66] We all have a past of regretful behaviors, actions or words. Like a sprinter loses speed when he looks back to gauge his competition, so looking back at moments of regret will hinder our forward progress spiritually, giving those regrets continued power over us. Pressing on with eyes fixed on the future, however, gives us the best chance to finish the race well.

This principle–forgetting the past and looking ahead to the future–provided the premise for Coach Yow's exercise. Physically burying all the negative things that happened the first half of the season produced a compelling visual reminder for the players to forget their previous games and move forward–refusing to allow the past to impede their progress. This simple activity propelled them to on-court success, but more importantly it taught them a practical principle to help them finish well in life.

31

Attitude of Gratitude

Liz Bailey Ham
NC State Wolfpack, 2001-2004

WOLFPACK HISTORY

The summer before my freshman year at NC State a teammate and I moved into the dorms, our exciting journey as Wolfpack basketball players about to begin. This same teammate gave me a journal with a Bible verse on the cover: "My grace is sufficient for you, my strength is made perfect in weakness."[67] That journal accompanied me on every road trip of my college career and holds many precious memories. Coach Yow led, motivated and coached us every day with her passion about life, basketball and faith influencing her every move.

Once, after a long day of class and practice, I went to the coaches offices to voice my frustration regarding my playing time. I worked so hard in practice, knew I could contribute in games and yet couldn't understand why I seemingly didn't get a chance. I sat down in Coach Yow's office decorated with team pictures from every year, trophies, awards and NC State paraphernalia galore. Looking around, I noticed the individual 8 x 10 photos of each member of our team that year, and it began to sink in—I was incredibly blessed to be a small part of Wolfpack women's basketball history and this special family. Coach Yow and I talked, but our conversation took on a broader scope than my playing time issue. We discussed the positive things that I could gain from being part of a team. Coach Yow listed things that I hadn't thought about and slowly, like the sun burning off the morning haze, I saw the real issue: I had become selfish.

Coach Yow reminded me that being part of a team isn't about

personal achievements like points scored or minutes played. She motivated me to change my outlook and attitude by embracing my role as a Christian leader on the team and enjoying every moment as an ACC player. That day is etched in both my mind and my journal where I wrote: *work on being selfless instead of selfish, be a team player, encourage others in their faith and, most importantly, be thankful for this opportunity God has given me.* Coach Yow taught me the power of an attitude of gratitude.

As I watched Coach Yow battle cancer, I saw her live out this same principle. Standing on the bedrock of her faith, she quickly offered thanks for her many blessings. As I think back to the verse on my journal, "my strength is made perfect in weakness," I realize that she embodied this as well, every day manifesting God's amazing strength when she felt weak.

My teammate who gave me the journal wrote a little note on the front page thanking me for telling her about God because, as a result, she had given control of her life to Jesus. I smile and thank God and Coach Yow, who once explained to me what it means to know God through Christ and set the stage for me to do the same with my teammate.

WOLFPACK WISDOM

Always be joyful. Never stop praying. Be thankful in all circumstances, for this is God's will for you who belong to Christ Jesus.

1 Thessalonians 5:16-18

The three-pound command center we call our brain carries a ton of power. The thoughts we permit to enter and settle there steer our lives much like a rudder directs a vessel. We face new situations each day–some exciting, some difficult and many beyond the scope of our control. Yet the one thing we can control, as Coach Yow preached many times, is the attitude with which we approach the rollercoaster of life. "Attitude is the key to success," she told decades of Wolfpack women. Our thoughts determine our attitude, so one way to maintain a good attitude is to "be thankful everyday"–another of Coach Yow's sayings that she gleaned from the Scriptures.

In the above verse, Paul instructs the Thessalonians to "Be thankful in all circumstances." Note that he doesn't say be thankful *for* all circumstances, but *in* them. It's tough to be thankful *for* the loss of a job, a loved one's diagnosis, or your child's addiction to drugs. Yet, with God's help, it's possible to be thankful *in the midst* of those situations. It's a matter of mindset and focus. Like Coach Yow, Paul preached principles he knew from experience.

On Paul's second missionary journey, he and Silas were beaten with rods and thrown in jail, their feet fastened in stocks. Rather than sulking in disbelief that the God they served would allow them such mistreatment, "...Paul and Silas were praying and singing hymns of praise to God..."[68] Ever tried praying and singing hymns in the midst of heartache and adversity? First, it's a choice–not something we're naturally inclined to do. Second, it's virtually impossible to do either and remain downcast. Choosing to turn our heart, mind and even face toward God while traversing the valleys of life causes a mental, emotional and spiritual shift. Our issues suddenly seem small when thrown up against the landscape of a vast and powerful God.

Choosing the attitude of gratitude is like looking through rose-colored glasses. Everything shows up in a different hue, bringing brightness and hope to the picture. We notice the sparkle of something good in the midst of the tragic. We see a blessing right there with the pain. Liz sat disgruntled in Coach Yow's office, but the photos and Wolfpack history around her opened her eyes to the privilege of being a Wolfpack woman. Her situation hadn't changed–she was still frustrated with her playing time–but her viewpoint had. Then, talking with Coach Yow revealed perspectives on leadership and opportunity that she hadn't considered. There, intermingled with her pain and disappointment, resided blessings she hadn't noticed.

Coach Yow lived with an attitude of gratitude. As if the coaching profession didn't offer enough opportunities to practice, her personal life proved an even tougher training ground. Weeks of chemo didn't sway her resolve. The heavy side effects that took her hair, caused her nails to fall off and put sores in her mouth didn't deter her from mining every day in search of God's blessings. She told anyone who would listen about them–God's love and salvation, her biological and Wolfpack families, prayers and letters of encouragement from both friends and strangers, the opportunity to help people, the Kay Yow/WBCA Cancer Fund–these blessings and many, many more sustained Coach Yow's rose-colored view of her cancer.

Sometimes a thankful heart expressed to God causes him to intervene and change our situation. During Paul and Silas' praise session a massive earthquake shook the prison to its foundation causing all the cell doors to fly open, their chains to fall off and their eventual release. But other times, like with Coach Yow, a thankful heart simply changes us. Her attitude of gratitude not only brought light to her soul, but like a magnet it attracted others to that light, showing scores of people the power of choosing to be thankful.

32

Bumps in the Road

Billie McDowell
NC State Wolfpack, 2002-2006

WOLFPACK HISTORY

My dream of playing basketball in college started during grade school when my parents took me to the recreation center to teach me how to dribble and shoot. I never imagined that one day I would play for someone who would impact my life to the degree that Coach Kay Yow did. Coach Yow taught me to never give up, to fight for what I believe in and to push past my own personal pain to overcome any obstacle.

My junior year at NC State was a break-out year for me. My points per game average increased from three as a sophomore to 12 as a junior, earning me 2nd team All-ACC honors. I found my rhythm in the NCAA tournament games–my three's were falling, my offensive penetration created openings for my teammates and our teamwork felt seamless. I felt sure this was our year to make it to the Final Four. Then, my biggest fear as an athlete happened. I tore my anterior cruciate ligament.

Talk about disappointment and fear! I thought my basketball career was over. After surgery, I remembered Coach Yow's wisdom: never give up, fight for what you believe in and push past your own personal pain to overcome any obstacle. These inspirational words gave birth to the determined and courageous spirit that kept me going.

Coach Yow often encouraged us to not allow bumps in the road to stop us from achieving our goals. Rather, she said, use that bump as a motivator to continue pressing on. Injuring my knee was a major bump in my road, but I was determined to return to the court a better player before. So 2-3 times a day I entered rehab with a positive attitude and gave 100% effort.

With God on my side and the support from my family, teammates, and coaches, I overcame my injury and returned for my senior year to contribute to the success of my team. The Wolfpack family is extravagant–full of loving, caring and reliable individuals. Yet it would have been incomplete without the right leader, without Coach Yow. She represented the cornerstone of our Wolfpack family.

Coach Yow was a big-time role model to me. She, too, traversed dark valleys and encountered bumps in the road. And through it all, she lived out the same principles she taught her players for so many years: never give up, fight for what you believe in and push past your own personal pain to overcome any obstacle.

WOLFPACK WISDOM

Each time he said, "My grace is all you need. My power works best in weakness." So now I am glad to boast about my weaknesses, so that the power of Christ can work through me. That's why I take pleasure in my weaknesses, and in the insults, hardships, persecutions, and troubles that I suffer for Christ. For when I am weak, then I am strong.

2 Corinthians 12:9-10

After the apostle Paul's conversion experience on the road to Damascus, he dedicated his life to telling people about Jesus. He traveled hundreds of miles to teach about Jesus and encouraged Christians everywhere to stand firm in their faith. Surely God would protect a man so tirelessly committed to spreading his message. Certainly a just and loving God would exempt his faithful servant Paul, from suffering.

Not so. In fact, of all the saints none were as acquainted with suffering as Paul. Beaten, shipwrecked, stoned and left for dead...he experienced all kinds of suffering. Just prior to the verses above, Paul tells the Corinthians about his affliction with a "thorn in [his] flesh"– an unknown physical condition that brought him pain and distress. He pleaded for God to remove it. But as God often does, he chose to change Paul's situation not by removing the thorn, but by giving Paul what he needed to endure the suffering–grace.

Grace is God's provision for our need right when we need it.[69] Paul experienced God's grace numerous times, as did Coach Yow. She could never have lived out the mantra she spoke into Billie's life–*Never give up, fight for what you believe in and push past your own personal pain to overcome any obstacle*–without an ongoing infusion of God's grace.

God's message to Paul spoke of sufficient grace. "My grace is all you need," he responded each time Paul pleaded for relief. God didn't give Paul an explanation, but rather a promise to provide enough grace for him to endure the suffering. And God's message spoke of strengthening grace. When Paul felt weak from his suffering, God's grace ushered in the strength necessary to see him through. "My power works best in weakness," God said.

This probably wasn't the message Paul wanted to hear, nor is it what we want to hear in the face of our own suffering. We want God to answer by eliminating our suffering. We want health to replace sickness and prosperity to replace poverty. We maneuver through life seeking to erase, or at least minimize, suffering. Yet to God, suffering has transforming purpose.

Think of a world without suffering–one absent of difficulties or challenges. We would roll through life unscathed and perhaps happy, but stagnant. Like it or not, suffering produces growth. Both Paul and Coach Yow knew this, and as a result they viewed suffering not as a curse, but as a gift–an opportunity for personal transformation. Suffering became the conduit through which they experienced God's sufficient and strengthening grace at a depth they'd previously not known. His grace sustained them, helping them rise above their suffering.

Through God's grace Paul could boast about his weaknesses, rejoicing and thanking God for them. His focus no longer rested on the inconvenience, pain or distress, but rather on God's purpose. Paul recognized how unmistakable God's power appeared to the watching world through his suffering and took pleasure in being a vessel through which others could see God work. Similarly, Coach Yow thanked God for her cancer–her bump in the road. She focused not on her discomfort, side-effects or pain, but on all the good that God produced in her life and in the lives of others because of her cancer. And that perspective set the stage for the watching world to see God's power as he infused her daily with his remarkably sufficient and strengthening grace, helping her to never give up, to fight for what she believed in and to push past her own personal pain to overcome any obstacle.

33

Coach Yow Ways

Rachel Stockdale
NC State Wolfpack, 2001-2006

WOLFPACK HISTORY

Reflecting back to my Wolfpack woman days,
Remembering the "Coach Yow Ways"…

Fresh pedicure–stars and stripes on a big toe,
Sporting her favorite black sandals, while she ran the show.
Actively involved, running the drills and working the court,
The staff always encouraging her to wear shoes during this sport.

But day in and day out, the black sandals she wore,
Tripping several times, but never hitting the floor.
Until the day she tripped… gracefully fell…face to the floor–
Finally, the request for her to put on shoes, she did not ignore!
(at least for the rest of that practice)

Now to the islands off the coast of Greece,
Where the baklava drips with the syrup so sweet.
And the rocks along the shore welcome visitors seeking a thrill–
Where players and support staff were jumping at will.

One by one, into the sea, people took the plunge,
And then the chants started when all were done–
There was only one person left….
"Coach Yow! Coach Yow! Coach Yow!" was the request.

She made her way to the edge of the rock, and looked into the sea–
glanced back at the chanting spectators, with the expression of,
"who, me?"

Off she went, over the edge to cheers and laughter all around,
The one and only Coach Kay Yow… she never let us down.

34

Positively Comforting

Monica Pope
NC State Wolfpack, 2002-2006

WOLFPACK HISTORY

At the beginning of my senior year, my father was diagnosed with colon cancer. On a three-way call, he gave my sisters and me the news. In the midst of my shock and disbelief, I tried to remain strong for my family–especially my sisters who took the news hard. That same year Coach Yow's cancer reoccurred. She brought the team together to tell us, and when she announced that she needed to take a leave of absence from coaching–even missing the Carolina game–we knew the seriousness of her condition.

During those moments in the locker room, Coach Yow spoke only positive words. She quoted the Bible, and though tears streamed down the cheeks of every player and coach, she remained strong. After the meeting, I called my father to encourage him with her words.

Everyday before or after practice, we received an update on Coach Yow's condition. We learned about her chemo treatments, her diet and generally how she felt. I shared what I knew about Coach Yow's experiences with my dad, and could tell–even through the phone–that it encouraged and inspired him to believe *if she can do it, I can too* and *if she can stay positive and still thank God for every moment, then I can too.*

Things happen for a reason and people come into our lives for a specific purpose. Coach Yow's positive spirit left an indelible mark not only on my life, but also on my dad's. Though his battle with cancer continues, he remains positive. Most importantly, he allowed God to become the leader of his life. He always used to ask about

Coach Yow's health and I'd tell him that she was still smiling in her favorite spot (under the basket).

WOLFPACK WISDOM

God is our merciful Father and the source of all comfort. He comforts us in all our troubles so that we can comfort others. When they are troubled, we will be able to give them the same comfort God has given us.
                                                                2 Corinthians 1:3b-4

The book of Acts documents the growth of the church after Jesus' death and resurrection. Jesus commissioned his closest followers (disciples) to take his message to their city, country and ultimately to the ends of the earth.[70] As a result, churches began popping up in villages, towns and cities throughout a region that spanned thousands of miles.

The young believers in these small congregations were unsure of how to grow in their faith, susceptible to following false teaching and tempted to return to their old way of life. The disciples traveled throughout Judea, Samaria and eventually the entire Roman Empire to share the Good News about Jesus with those who had never heard it and to offer comfort and encouragement to those who had already believed–many of whom had been scattered due to persecution. Despite the trials they encountered (imprisonment, beatings and the like) the disciples held tightly to their faith and encouraged others to do the same. God had given them a purpose and they intended to carry it out regardless of the opposition.

Coach Yow lived the same way. When her cancer returned, she asked God to show her his purpose in it. "I just can't see going through it…just going through it for nothing or for myself," she said. "As time went by, the Lord graciously showed me a purpose."[71] Coach Yow's faith empowered her to comfort, encourage and inspire others affected by cancer (like Monica's dad) to keep fighting…to keep living.

The word translated *encourage* in some New Testament verses means "a calling to one's aid or to one's side."[72] God never meant for us to go through life solo. From the beginning, he reasoned that it wasn't good for man to be alone, creating Eve to live alongside Adam. As long as humanity exists, in good times and in bad, we will need others to come to our side.

Another common meaning of *encourage* is to comfort or console[73], as Paul describes in these verses from 2 Corinthians:

> *For the more we suffer for Christ, the more God will shower us with his comfort through Christ. Even when we are weighed down with troubles, it is for your comfort and salvation! For when we ourselves are comforted, we will certainly comfort you. Then you can patiently endure the same things we suffer. We are confident that as you share in our sufferings, you will also share in the comfort God gives us. (2 Corinthians 1:5-7)*

These words so aptly describe the encouragement Coach Yow spread to others. She became a source of comfort because she first experienced comfort from God. The more she suffered, the more comfort God poured out and the more she gave away. Her personal experience of all the emotions that came with cancer combined with her genuine, compassionate heart brought her alongside people in a way that imparted comfort.

From people within the Wolfpack family to those she never met, Coach Yow fulfilled God's purpose for her cancer through the encouragement and comfort she offered to thousands of people through her words, her actions and her very life.

35

Every Role Matters

Danielle Wilhelm
NC State Wolfpack, 2005-2007

WOLFPACK HISTORY

In 2005, I transferred to NC State after playing two years at South Plains Junior College. That first year at State I struggled with my role on the team and as the season went on, the coaches met with me a number of times to explain the importance of my role and the value I brought to our team. Coach Yow knew just the right words to encourage me and consistently made me feel like my contribution was just as important as shooting the last-second shot at the end of a championship game. She taught me to be proud of my place on the team and to be the best role player possible, even though my responsibilities went unnoticed and unrewarded much of the time.

Going into my senior year, Coach Yow met with me and explained my role on that year's team in great detail. She encouraged my participation in various leadership organizations and conferences to help me learn how to lead well from my position as a role player. Later that year when Coach Yow had to take a leave of absence from the team, she pushed me to become an even stronger leader. After she broke the news to us about the resurgence of her cancer and her impending leave of absence, I said, "Don't worry Coach Yow, I will be your extra voice during games and practices." She smiled at me and said, "I know you will." At that moment, I got it. I finally understood that I didn't have to be the star player to have an impact on our team.

Through her passion and love for both people and basketball, Coach Yow taught me how to take what life gives me and make the absolute best of it, because for some reason it was meant for me. I carry with me the knowledge that many roles exist in both basketball and life, and each holds equal importance in God's eyes. Now, as a basketball coach myself, this lesson colors how I view and treat my own players. I push every player equally, forcing them to better themselves even if I know they won't play in the next game. Following the example of Coach Yow, I seek to teach each player that regardless of her role, she matters to both me and the team.

WOLFPACK WISDOM

The human body has many parts, but the many parts make up one whole body. So it is with the body of Christ...and God has put each part just where he wants it.

1 Corinthians 12:12, 18

Like many college athletes, Danielle struggled to accept her role on the Wolfpack team. Transitions challenge the best of us, and most high school stars or junior college transfers entering college programs experience big adjustments with roles, expectations and undoubtedly, playing time. Such a common point of discontent, college coaches must tire of discussing playing time issues with their athletes. Yet, Coach Yow's interactions with Danielle modeled not only patience, but also the ability to capitalize on teachable moments.

The concept of teamwork makes participation in sports a crucible for lessons about life. No matter where we go, most of us spend at least some time as part of a team. With family or at work, school or church–life holds countless opportunities to work alongside others to achieve a goal. Intellectually we know that the strength of any team lies in the distinct gifts that each person brings to bear and how those gifts complement one another to make the team unit stronger than its individual parts. Yet sometimes we become discontent with our role and want a different one–perhaps one with more power or prestige. That discontentment hurts the team, making it harder for it to achieve its objectives.

The apostle Paul used the metaphor of the human body in 1 Corinthians 12 to show how the parts of a team were meant to operate. Our bodies are amazing machines. When operating smoothly, every part complements the other, working together to help us breathe, eat, think, talk and move. It's simply unbelievable how many little muscles and organs must do their jobs so that our bodies work! Did you know, for example, that it takes 17 muscles to smile and 43 to frown? Or that if the pineal gland (one of our smallest organs–the size of a pea) doesn't function properly it will affect our ability to sleep? We may think that some parts carry more importance than others, but any doctor will remind us how crucial every part is for the human body to function properly. Paul put it this way:

> *If the foot says, "I am not a part of the body because I am not a hand," that does not make it any less a part of the body. And if the ear says, "I am not part of the body because I am not an eye," would that make it any less a part of the body? If the whole body were an eye, how would you hear? Or if your whole body were an ear, how would you smell anything?*
>
> *But our bodies have many parts, and God has put each part just where he wants it. How strange a body would be if it had only one part! Yes, there are many parts, but only one body. The eye can never say to the hand, "I don't need you." The head can't say to the feet, "I don't need you."(1 Corinthians 12:15-21)*

The same holds true for any team! In basketball, the point guard can't say to the center, "I don't need you." At work, the department director can't tell her assistant, "I don't need you." At school, the janitor can't think, "I'm not a part of the staff here because I'm not the principal." The basketball team's rebounding edge would likely disappear without the center and the department director would surely miss some appointments without her assistant. As unseen as a janitor may feel, schools would suffer without his contribution. The bottom line? We need one another.

We tend to associate the more visible roles with greater importance, but both Paul and Coach Yow would disagree. Both taught that no matter what a person's role–seen or unseen, high profile or low–no team will reach its potential unless every part does its job.

36

Carolina Connection

Jane Albright
Head Coach
University of Nevada, Reno

WOLFPACK INFLUENCE

Over the years Kay and I developed a special friendship. In fact, she traditionally joined my family for Christmas dinner each year in my hometown of Graham, North Carolina. Time with her marked one of the highlights of our holiday! Her stories captivated my whole family and her gifts–she always brought something special to my mother and two elderly aunts–meant so much. On Christmas 2006, when Kay was right in the middle of her fight with cancer, we were all scared she would not be able to come, but late that day she arrived, once again bearing special stories and gifts.

Kay rarely talked about herself, but this Christmas she spoke of her battle with cancer and the hundreds of letters she had received from people who had prayed for her and wanted to encourage her. As she talked I could tell she was burdened, and then she explained that she didn't have the energy to respond to each letter, and she so wanted to. I quickly told her that all of these people, most of whom didn't know her personally, did not expect an answer to their words. "But I at least want to answer the young people's letters," she said. "You know, letter writing is a dying thing now and I want to encourage them to write more of them."

Only Kay Yow would take something meant just for her and turn it back to the giver. I didn't argue because I understood that this attitude was Kay. It showed the very servant heart that made her Kay Yow. When she left that Christmas, I was especially thankful that she came by, for many times Christ's best gifts are wrapped in a person. That, for sure, was always true with Kay.

A couple of springs ago, I was in North Carolina visiting my mother and Kay came by to eat barbeque with my family. When she came to the door, I was taken aback, as she was completely bald. The cancer had robbed her of her beautiful crown of hair. Usually Kay wore a wig when undergoing chemo, so this picture of her was different than the one I had known for 30 years. Of course no one said a thing, we were just glad to see her. About a half-hour into the visit, Kay grasped her head and exclaimed, "I forgot my hair!" and jumped up to go get it. Seems that on the ride to Graham, it was pretty hot! Of course we told her to forget it–that she was fine. Actually, we were honored that she came in without her wig.

We proceeded to eat and my nephew Jonathan, a high school senior, casually asked if we knew where he could get his wrinkled tuxedo pressed. We did, of course, but then the clincher–he needed it that night! Kay asked me to get her an iron and something in the way she asked told me not to argue. Jonathan got out his guitar, and as he serenaded us to *Piano Man*, Kay ironed his tuxedo. We all began singing and dancing around the room as Jon played and Kay ironed. I will always remember that afternoon! Here stood one of the most prolific coaches in the country, battling cancer and ironing my nephew's tuxedo simply because it needed ironing. My friend Kay and her servant heart–no one did it better.

37

We Can Do This

Sherri Coale
Head Coach
University of Oklahoma

WOLFPACK INFLUENCE

When I was president of the Women's Basketball Coaches Association (WBCA) one of my many tasks was to preside over the yearly convention held at the Final Four. Unfortunately for a coach, the Final Four is slightly less than fabulous unless, of course, you're playing in it. The pageantry surrounding it serves as a fastidious reminder of your ineptitude. To be president of your coaches association and not be playing is to sit in the anti-catbird seat. That was my lot in April 2008. Nonetheless, I flew to Tampa with my upper lip stiff and my game face tightly screwed on. My goal was to take care of business, do my job, and return unscathed. I can still hear Meatloaf singing, "Two out of three ain't bad."

One part of my job was to address the various women's basketball entities who meet at the convention–high school coaches, junior college coaches, Division II and III coaches, male coaches of women's basketball, black coaches of women's basketball–the president makes the rounds. And here's where I failed to return unscathed. As I went from body to body explaining what the WBCA does–how it can serve, why all coaches are important, how everyone matters–I got drenched in the juju of Kay Yow.

Let me explain. In 2008, our coaches association set out to raise significant funds for research and awareness in the fight against breast cancer. This insidious disease attacks one in every seven females. In our profession that means your neighbor. On a basketball team, that means at least two from every single squad will fight this monster for their lives. When one of our own had to rise up to battle for the third time, it was the ultimate teachable moment. Coach Kay Yow's personal fight became our professional war. Through the indefatigable efforts of the WBCA CEO, Beth Bass, and her staff, within a year's time the Kay Yow/WBCA Cancer Fund was real and we had raised over one million dollars.

Coach Yow was certainly not the first or the only NCAA Division I head basketball coach battling cancer, but her fight was undoubtedly the wind beneath our wings. Coach was one of those rare competitors whom nobody hated. And that was true before she got sick.

Coach Yow not only let the world watch her fight cancer, she invited us to. She allowed us to witness her living with the disease, refusing to bow down to it. She coached bald wearing the coolest chandelier earrings in town, she coached in a wig with band-aids covering the tips of her fingers where nails used to be, and she coached in a white Nike sweat suit with a big pink ribbon sewn on the chest. She even took chemo on a plane en route to coach an NCAA tournament game. We admired her fight so much that we wore pink shoes and gave away pink shirts and played with pink basketballs trying to say, "You are not out there alone. A nation of coaches has your back and we will not go quietly."

As I made my way through meeting after meeting at the Final Four, I was absolutely moved by how the countenance of the room changed when I began to speak about the *Pink Zone* campaign and the potential impact of the Kay Yow/WBCA Cancer Fund. It happened every time. Whatever the level, whatever the issues, whatever the size of the group—the Kay Yow cause galvanized the room. I watched the most competitive people on the planet shed their own selfish skins and lock arms for a cause outside themselves and I was reminded of what it is that makes this thing we do so great.

We fight. Like little rabid, stubborn dogs, we fight. Some of what we fight over and for is infantile and purposeless. Sometimes it matters but it's not important. And then along comes Kay Yow and the fog lifts. And we get permission, in an almost spiritual sense, to do what we do best. Together. All on the same team.

What our "nation of coaches" did in year one of the creation of the Fund is remarkable. Even the folks at our parent non-profit, the renowned JimmyV Foundation, were stunned. So after a fabulous start, what's the ultimate goal? Over a plate of nachos in Augusta, Georgia in August 2008, Kay made it sound so simple. We raise $5 million in 2009. She had the mathematical formula for doing it down pat. She even spouted the numbers in the multiplication tree–and scientific lingo was so not her bag. Then we fund the researcher who finds the cure for breast cancer, she said. And every women's basketball coach in America will be a part of that. It becomes painfully clear that THAT was almost as cool to her as finding the cure itself.

One of Kay's favorite stories was one about a rural high school near Raleigh that raised $2,500 at their high school girl's *Pack the Place Pink* basketball game one fall. The young lady who led the charge was a freshman. She told Coach Yow that not only would they raise even more money in the future, but that she would train someone to lead it once she graduated. The Fund could count on their money from now on. Coach Yow's face just glowed when she told that story, and I could never quite tell if it was the concept of exponential expansion of what every little team in America could do financially to fuel the research for finding a cure, or if it was the fighting spunk of this little self-appointed leader that lit her fire.

When Kay Yow talked about the *Pink Zone* and the development of the next stage of the Fund, you almost forgot the enemy had taken outposts in her blood. Her faith in God, in her doctors, in medicine, in people and in her profession was profound. As she paused between nachos to swallow her newest knight in shining armor–the chemotherapy pill–she seemed almost giddy at the thought of what could be.

"Just one person can make such a difference," she said, her voice dripping in Carolina drawl. "We can do this." And with that thought my shoulders rose and I recognized in myself what I had seen repeatedly in coaches at the Final Four. In fighting for Kay and a million other women like her, we play our very best game.

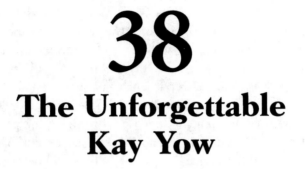

38

The Unforgettable
Kay Yow

Jim Davis
Head Coach
Clemson University
1987-2005

WOLFPACK INFLUENCE

Several years ago, when we played host to NC State, my 86 year-old mother was visiting and attended the game. I told Coach Yow that I wanted her to meet Mom. She graciously came down from the locker room and suddenly I found myself in the presence of two of the most godly women I've ever known. I told Coach Yow that we never lost when Mom came to our games and she promptly asked her, "Do you pray for Jim's team to win?" Of course Mom replied, "Oh no! I just pray that they play their best and that no one will get hurt."

When on the road during summer recruiting, Coach Yow and I always tried to go to dinner a few times. One year, while in Washington, D.C. we decided to get an early start to eat at The Cheesecake Factory, one of her favorite restaurants. Upon arrival, we parked on the street directly in front of the restaurant amidst some other cars. After about an hour-and-a-half (we had to have the cheesecake), we came out and the parking spot had turned into a traffic lane during rush hour! Remarkably, no one hit our car. We later realized we parked beside a sign reading, "No parking between the hours of 4:30 and 6:30 p.m." but we didn't even get a ticket. You never got in trouble when you were in the company of Kay Yow!

Clearly, the pioneers of ACC women's basketball are Coach

Debbie Ryan of Virginia, Coach Chris Weller of Maryland, and of course, Coach Kay Yow. One year at the ACC spring meetings, the women's basketball coaches wrestled over issues to present to the ACC Athletic Directors and Faculty Representatives (FAR's). No issue was an "easy sell." This particular year we wanted to move to three officials. We knew the AD's and FAR's response may not be favorable and we nominated Coach Yow to make the presentation the next day. Kay knew a veteran Major League Baseball umpire whom she called for advice.

The next day, with passion and enthusiasm, Kay explained how baseball umpires stand in position with their hands on their knees and their head still in order to get a good look at every play. I can still see Kay emulating that umpire's stance! She argued that adding a third official would allow all three officials to get a good look at each play, virtually eliminating the need to make calls on the run. The AD's and FAR's voted unanimously to allow the ACC to go to three officials. Their respect for Coach Yow (not to mention her passionate presentation) made the ACC the first conference to approve three-man crews for women's basketball. Even after years as a coach, Kay Yow was still pioneering!

39

An Unbreakable Bond

Sylvia Hatchell
Head Coach
University of North Carolina

WOLFPACK INFLUENCE

When I first started coaching at Francis Marion College back in 1975, we had a small budget and no basketball shoes. Kay Yow had a contract with George Lehmann and Pro Keds and I met her at one of their clinics. I told Kay about my situation at Francis Marion and asked if she could get me a discount on shoes for my team. The next week, Kay called me and said that since our colors were Red, White and Blue, she would send me some red and white shoes from her NC State allotment. Kay insisted on gifting them to us and wouldn't accept any money. Her act of kindness sparked what became a close friendship.

During the next few years, Kay and I spent time on various Women's Basketball Coaches Association and USA Basketball committees. In 1985, Kay asked me to be her assistant coach for the Good Will Games and the World Championships to be held the summer of 1986 in Russia. We got into trouble for taking Bibles into a communist country, but still won two gold medals.

Kay and I were roommates on a USA Basketball trip when the University of North Carolina, NC State's No. 1 rival, named me their new coach. When I told Kay, she said, "Oh no!"

"Kay," I said, "we can handle this, it will be O.K."

"Sylvia, I know we can handle this," she replied, "it's our fans who won't understand!"

In 1987, Kay was named the 1988 USA Olympic Coach and

once again, asked me to be her assistant. During the summer of '87, while enjoying the swimming pool at Pat Summit's house, Pat received a call from Nora Lynn Finch telling us that Kay had breast cancer. Obviously this would affect Kay's travel schedule during our preparation for the Olympics. Though I had just taken the job at UNC and knew it would take lots of extra work to build the program, I decided to dedicate my time to USA Basketball and helping Kay win a gold medal. Although this delayed my progress at UNC, I made the right choice.

Throughout our coaching careers, Kay and I competed hard against one another, and yet remained close friends because of our faith and the friendship we forged in the early years of the WBCA and USA Basketball. We experienced amazing moments: laughing, crying, winning and losing our rivalry games, winning gold medals, visiting the demilitarized zone in Korea, attending church in many foreign countries and sharing our faith. Although Kay and I coached at rival schools, our Christian faith gave us a sisterhood–a bond and a love that could NEVER be broken.

40

The Purpose Driven Life

Debbie Ryan
Head Coach
University of Virginia

WOLFPACK INFLUENCE

I knew Kay Yow since the beginning of my coaching career 32 years ago. She epitomized what a coach should be in both demeanor and action. Kay was the kinder, gentler version of today's women's basketball coach.

As a young coach I learned the finer points of professionalism from Kay. She definitely helped to shape me as both a woman and a professional. I remember getting over-zealous in making a point at league meetings only to catch a look of disappointment from Kay. That was all it took for me to realize I crossed a line and needed to change my approach.

Kay always knew how to express her passion in a way that made a huge impact on others. Early on, Kay passionately advocated television coverage of women's basketball. Her impact on this issue was felt beyond North Carolina and even the Southeast, as she influenced athletic directors nationwide.

You cannot speak about Kay Yow without mentioning her spirituality. It permeated every cell in her body. She lived the purpose driven life. An inspirational storyteller, Kay wove a life-changing lesson into every story that she told. She was one-of-a-kind and just meeting her could change a young person's life forever.

Kay's dedication, spirit and enthusiasm for life colored everything she did. As one of the most memorable and influential people I've known, she left many indelible imprints on my life. She taught me how to embrace and express humility, to have passion for what I believe in and to show empathy for those in our profession.

41

My Mom's Favorite Coach

Chris Weller
Head Coach
University of Maryland
1975-2002

WOLFPACK INFLUENCE

Kay and I were longtime competitors and friends–we coached in the ACC in the early years. The NC State–Maryland rivalry was one of the strongest in the ACC. We fought against each other in games, but worked alongside each other on issues related to the growth of women's basketball both in the ACC and nationally. Our families supported us and one another too. Kay's dad, Hilton, would always sit and talk to me before our games against the Wolfpack, and my mom always admired Kay.

In 1984 my mom had a severe stroke. Kay wrote her a beautiful letter and sent her flowers. That gesture of kindness meant so much to my mom as she battled though a year of rehabilitation. After that, she always referred to Kay as her favorite coach.

As you might imagine, I showed some concern when my mom made this declaration to everyone–including the "Rebounders" (our Maryland booster club). "Mom, what about me," I'd say. She would laugh and say, "You know what I mean." Fortunately, I did know what she meant. She admired Kay's ethics, kindness and thoughtfulness, as did I. Kay became more than just my mom's favorite coach, she became one of her favorite people as well.

Notes

[1] Romans 8:28

[2] See Genesis 37-47

[3] Genesis 39:2

[4] adopt. Dictionary.com. *Dictionary.com Unabridged (v 1.1)*. Random House, Inc. http://dictionary1.classic.reference.com/browse/adopt (accessed: May 12, 2009).

[5] Romans 8:17; Matthew 25:34

[6] Titus 1:2; 1 Peter 1:4

[7] Acts 16:1-3

[8] 1 Timothy 1:3

[9] Adapted from *Discover God Study Bible*. Tyndale House Publishers (2007) p.2178

[10] 2 Timothy 1:14b

[11] 2 Timothy 3:16

[12] 2 Timothy 3:11-12

[13] 2 Timothy 2:2

[14] Hebrews 9:22

[15] *A Final Farewell*, Gravitation Studios (2009)

[16] Joshua 7

[17] Joshua 9

[18] Joshua 10:25

[19] Daniel 1:4

[20] Daniel 1:8a

[21] Daniel 1:11-15

[22] Daniel 2:47

[23] Daniel 2:48

[24] Daniel 6:4

[25] Daniel 6:10b

[26] Nehemiah 2:17, emphasis mine

[27] 1 Samuel 9:2

[28] Luke 12:48b

[29] Philippians 4:13

[30] John 1:1-3

[31] John 15:13

[32] humility. (n.d.). *Webster's Revised Unabridged Dictionary.* Retrieved May 12, 2009, from Dictionary.com website: http://dictionary1.classic.reference.com/browse/humility

[33] *Pride, Passion & Power.* ESPN (2009)

[34] *Pride, Passion & Power.* ESPN (2009)

[35] John 14:27

[36] Romans 8:28 (NIV)

[37] Philippians 1:12b

[38] *Heart of a Coach Breakfast.* Fellowship of Christian Athletes (2008)

[39] Genesis 6:9b

[40] Genesis 6:22

[41] Hebrews 11:8b

[42] *Sharing the Victory* interview. Fellowship of Christian Athletes (2008)

[43] Hebrews 11:35b

[44] Exodus 3:11b

[45] Exodus 4:10

[46] *Sharing the Victory* interview. Fellowship of Christian Athletes (2008)

[47] Philippians 3:17

[48] Titus 2:7

[49] Matthew 26:33

[50] Matthew 26:35

[51] Matthew 26:75

[52] John 4:17-18

[53] John 4:27

[54] Matthew 14:27

[55] Matthew 14:28

[56] Hebrews 12:1b-2a

[57] *Sharing the Victory* interview, Fellowship of Christian Athletes (2008)

[58] *Turn Your Eyes Upon Jesus,* by Helen H. Lemmel (1922) Public Domain

[59] Exodus 16

[60] Colossians 3:22

[61] 1 Samuel 17:26b

[62] hope. (2009). In *Merriam-Webster Online Dictionary.* Retrieved May 14, 2009, from http://www.merriam-webster.com/dictionary/hope

[63] *Discover God Study Bible,* Tyndale House Publishers (2007) p. 2344

[64] Matthew 27:51

[65] *The Bible Exposition Commentary Volume 2,* by Warren Wiersbe. SP Publications, Inc. (1989) p. 89

66 Wiersbe, p. 89

67 2 Corinthians 12:9 (NIV)

68 Acts 16:25

69 *The Bible Exposition Commentary Volume 1*, by Warren Wiersbe. SP Publications, Inc. (1989) p. 675

70 Acts 1:8

71 *Pride, Passion & Power*, ESPN (2009)

72 *The Expanded Vines Expository Dictionary*, by W.E. Vine. Bethany House Publishers (1984) p. 390

73 Vine, p. 356